COMEDY GOES TO COURT

When People Stop Laughing and Start Fighting

Carl Unegbu

Published by
Hybrid Global Publishing
333 E 14th Street
#3C
New York, NY 10003

Manufactured in the United States of America, or in the United Kingdom when distributed elsewhere.

Unegbu, Carl.
Comedy Goes to Court
        ISBN: 978-1-957013-31-2
        eBook: 978-1-957013-32-9
        LCCN: 2022906816

Cover design by: Natasha Clawson
Copyediting by: Dea Gunning
Interior design by: Suba Murugan
Author Photo by: Deborah Sanders

https://www.ocarlslaw.com

This book is dedicated to the comedy community everywhere and to all who love the comedy art form.

Contents

Acknowledgments

It has taken me a while to finally get this book published and, needless to say, this would not have been possible without the help and collaboration of many people along the way. First, I would like to give many thanks to Karen Strauss, the head of Hybrid Global, the publishing firm responsible for this book, and her team for their diligent and professional efforts in bringing this work to market. Karen's very capable team included my project managers Sara Foley and Karina Cooke; my developmental editor Claudia Volkman and my cover designer Natasha Clawson.

I would also like to thank comedian and journalist Travis Irvine, who was my co-host at the quarterly *Comedy Dialogue* series in the Upper West Side of Manhattan, which were pretty exciting hybrid events that regularly served up standup comedy bits and panel discussions. These series often illuminated some of the big issues in contemporary comedy and did certainly inform some of the stories covered in the book. Of course, I am also Immensely grateful to all the many attendees and friends of the series over the years for their enthusiasm about the events.

Also deserving of my thanks are attorney Carol Hauge and other friends and colleagues of mine for their moral support and encouragement in the writing of the book.

And, considering how the journey on this book all began, there is no forgetting to warmly thank the many readers of my blog *O'Carl's Law* for their comments and words of encouragement to me as a blogger over the years. I thank each and every single one of them very sincerely. As noted in the Introduction and Epilogue sections of this book, the blog was the inspiration for the book and, as everyone knows, without the readers a blog is nothing.

Thank you all very much.
Carl Unegbu

Introduction

This book is the culmination of a journey that began about ten years ago when I started writing a blog named *O'Carl's Law* (www.ocarlslaw.com). That was not long after I became an editor at *Comedybeat*, a website that covered comedy at the time. For me, launching the blog was purely a labor of love since my work on the blog was not intended as a money-making enterprise, and there was certainly no plan whatsoever to write a book. My only goal in starting the blog was to periodically provide a running commentary on the entertainment stories of the day, in a style so simple it would feel like an informal conversation between two pals hanging out in the bleachers at a New York Yankees baseball game. And as I began to focus my writing more on comedy industry events and controversies, I noticed that my growing audience was literally hanging on every word in each succeeding blog entry.

By their remarks in the "Comments" section of the blog, it was evident that most of my readers were very appreciative of what they described as the "easy" and "simple" style of the writing, which allowed them to understand and follow the complex and sometimes esoteric stuff being discussed in the posts. They often said they felt like I was having a conversation with them on many of the things they'd usually just wondered about. By this, the readers were referring to the way that comedians have to navigate the tricky intersection between two worlds that can seem to be at odds with one another—namely, the world of the law which tends to be restrictive in nature because it essentially regulates things and the world of the comedians themselves which, in contrast, tends to encourage permissiveness because of its rather edgy and sometimes "weird" nature.

I also realized that nobody else was writing about things like this—at least not that I could find. Then, about eight years ago, I released my first book *Comedy Under Attack: The Golden Age & the Headwinds*, and during a Q&A session at a book reading in New York City, a local comedian and a regular reader of my blog told me she thought it would be a great idea if my next book was based on the kinds of stuff that I wrote about on my blog.

As I thought about it more, the realization hit me that I was perhaps in a better position than most people to write a book of this kind. For starters, I covered comedy regularly as an editor at *Comedybeat*, which caused me to have frequent interactions with comedians and other industry players. Plus, I figured that being a lawyer also placed me in a good position to break down and explain many of the arcane legal stuff—or as some might put it, legal mumbo jumbo—in a way that, say, the average Joe riding the New York City subway could readily understand. I was determined early on not to allow myself to fall into the class of lawyers who, as a result of talking just like lawyers, unwittingly shut out non-lawyers from the conversation. In trying to avoid this pitfall, I came to rely quite heavily on my training and work as a journalist, which is a line of work that comes with a fair amount of storytelling skills.

Given my background, the content of this book doesn't contain any legal-format citations of the kind that I must concede, lawyers obsess about when they write. No citations of legal cases whatsoever! There are very few, if any, legal jargons or Latin words or phrases contained in the writings. My hope is that this book will be similarly reader-friendly, whether the reader is someone versed in the law or just a regular guy.

Concerning the arrangement of the book, each of the several legal cases or situations discussed in the book have been put under a broad category (or chapter) which describes the kinds of situations that are dealt with by the cases included in that chapter. Thus, there are such chapters as "Hashing out the Deal for Comedy Jobs;" "the Right of Comedians to Free Speech;" "Copying the Work or Appearance of Others"; "Comedians Getting in Trouble Onstage and Offstage;" "When the Funny Goes Silly;" "Divvying Up the Dollars from Comedy Work;" and finally, "The Intersection Crisis: Comedy & Other People's Lives." The beginning of each chapter contains a brief description of the kinds of subject matter covered by the cases or situations contained in that chapter.

Furthermore, though the popular imagination of comedy seems dominated by both the antics and the brilliance of stand-up comedians, it is worth noting that there is more to it than just stand-up comedy: the other genres include sketches, improvisations, and sitcoms. Considering this, I figured that it might be a good idea in a book of this nature to include some interesting situations that occur in other genres of comedy besides stand-up. So, I have included a few "pushing-and-shoving" situations from the sitcom world. For instance, one of the cases discussed in this book concerns the disagreement surrounding Charlie Sheen's messy exit from the hit CBS comedy *Two and a Half Men* in March 2011. Another case dealt with the money fight over Tim Allen's 1990s sitcom *Home Improvement*, which has since gone into syndication. Suffice it to say then that this book made a conscious decision to broaden its lens in an attempt to take in a fair selection of cases and situations in the world of comedy where people, as the subtitle of the book suggests, simply 'stop laughing and start fighting' instead.

Also, since many of the cases covered in the book were ongoing court cases at the time they were discussed in my blog, I deemed it a worthwhile idea, wherever appropriate and available, to give the readers a more complete picture of the entire situation by including "updates" on those cases. These updates provide information on how the cases were settled by the parties themselves or failing that, how the courts instead resolved the cases for them. Where no updates have been provided because no further recorded information exists, odds are that the cases are still pending or perhaps have been abandoned by the litigants themselves. Needless to say, that doesn't affect the validity of the legal principles controlling the situations as discussed in the stories.

Each case discussed in the book is preceded by the place where the events in the case took place, the date I originally posted the information on my blog, and the original content. Therefore, please note that the articles do not appear in chronological order, but rather according to the particular subject or topic that each article is illustrating.

In the end, in choosing to write this book, my intention is to offer it as a sort of service to the comedy industry: by illuminating some of the issues and circumstances that a lot of funny men and women seem to be struggling with in their professional lives. In a manner of speaking, who better to attempt this rather difficult task than someone whose background and experience appear to stand at the intersection of the worlds of comedy and the law?

HASHING OUT THE DEAL FOR COMEDY JOBS

CHAPTER ONE

HASHING OUT THE DEAL FOR COMEDY JOBS

As the opening chapter in the book, it seems appropriate to devote this section to the task of making the contracts and deals that allow comedians to get to work, whether stand-up comics or comedians who work in the sitcom world. Increasingly, as comedy settles into its "golden age" and comedians are recognized as true professionals who can make a genuine living doing what they enjoy doing, contracts will become increasingly utilized, much like entertainers in other fields such as acting and music. This chapter won't cover interactions that occur in less formal situations like open mics for stand-up comics. Such forums are not usually understood by comedy industry people as money-making situations: oftentimes, the open mics merely offer working comedians a forum for working on their material in order to polish them up and get them ready for actual paying gigs.

Most entertainers don't fully appreciate that many of the problems that come up in the course of their work could have been avoided by a careful wording of the agreements by which they are hired to perform in the first place. As the cases in this section show, sometimes the problem arises from something that wasn't said in the agreement, which should actually have been said.

Other times, the problem is about provisions inserted into the agreement or perhaps powers and rights given under the agreement in circumstances where the parties did not know at the outset just how such powers and rights might be used in the future. While no one has a crystal ball and something like this cannot be an exact science, the more clearly the agreement anticipates what problems could lurk around the corner and the more it fully covers the bases of the working relationship, the less there will be the potential for disputes, especially the very unnecessary ones. Now, let's get to the cases!

* * *

Avoiding Garry Shandling's Big Mistake

California
January 11, 2010

In 1998, comedian Garry Shandling and his then manager, Brad Grey, the current chairman and CEO of Paramount Studios in Hollywood had a major falling out, followed by a $100 million lawsuit by Shandling. Their long-term relationship collapsed over money issues surrounding the well-acclaimed HBO series *The Larry Sanders Show*, which ran between 1992 and 1998.

Claiming that he alone created and sold the show to HBO, Shandling accused Grey of "triple-dipping" on him by taking a half ownership of the show, snagging a producer's fee, and collecting commissions from Shandling's writing and acting fees.

Worse, Shandling claimed that when asked about the monies he was collecting, Grey threatened to make his life miserable and sent private detective, Anthony Pellicano, to snoop on his police records and plant smears against him. Pellicano himself ended up getting indicted by the Feds for racketeering and wiretapping.

In 1999, Grey paid $10 million to Shandling to settle the case at the last minute. But Shandling's mistake is a genuine teachable moment for entertainers with managers and agents.

For starters, Shandling apparently got himself a lawyer rather late in the game, only after Grey allegedly stonewalled his request for information about the monies. He needed a lawyer much sooner and here's why. Most managers tend to be long term pals of entertainers who trust them to provide the best career advice; promote the entertainers' careers and watch their backs for them. Sometimes, managers can double as agents by finding work and negotiating deals for the entertainers. Thus, managers can really loom pretty large in entertainers' professional lives.

But the flip side is that managers can and sometimes do abuse their position. So, the smarter thing is for the entertainer to protect himself first against his manager before having his manager protect him from the world. This means that the comedian ought to draw up a well-rounded contract with his manager, which would address most, if not all of the issues that can arise in their relationship going forward.

It cannot be said enough that despite the entertainer's bond of trust and affection for his buddy and manager, he needs to negotiate his contract with him at arms' length and this is where the entertainer could really use his high-prized lawyer to carry the buckets for him. To be sure, the relationship between the entertainer and his manager is one that would qualify as a "fiduciary" relationship in which the law tries to look out for the little guy. However, the law is not in the business of assisting people who have neglected their own affairs.

Above all, entertainers should make an effort to understand the terms of any contracts their managers are negotiating or signing on their behalf. Here, entertainers should "trust but verify." And this is important, because Shandling claimed that Grey would not even let him see the contracts he was negotiating with outsiders on Shandling's behalf and that Grey simply kept him on a "need to know" status. Big problem!

In negotiating the manager's contract, entertainers and their lawyers may perhaps want to follow a simple rule of thumb sometimes called the "officious bystander" rule, something that most English transactional lawyers would be familiar with. In the Shandling case here, one can perhaps imagine this [officious bystander] character as some busybody standing around while Grey and Shandling are negotiating their agreement, and although he has no assigned role in their negotiations, this character, being so officious, nonetheless proceeds to ask the negotiators whether, for instance, Grey would get any share of Shandling's writing and acting fees. If their [Grey and Shandling's] answer to that question is not exactly the same, then an expensive lawsuit is probably in their future, meaning that they still need to reach an agreement on that particular question, in order to avoid any trouble ahead.

The big lesson here is that what happened to Shandling didn't need to happen and as the saying goes, "a stitch in time saves nine."

COMEDY CENTRAL Versus DAVE CHAPPELLE: Lessons from a Standoff

New York
December 13, 2009

The year was 2004, comedian Dave Chappelle was ruling the comedy scene, and Comedy Central also wanted a piece of him. So, the network made him an offer he couldn't refuse. But less than a year later, he couldn't walk away from it fast enough as he dropped the gig like he'd been holding a red-hot stove.

Here's the story: In August 2004, Comedy Central's parent Viacom and the comedian inked an unprecedented $50 million deal, (which included a share of DVD sales), to continue the *Chappelle's Show* for two more years. The show had become a ratings jackpot for the network and its DVD sales were the highest of any TV show at the time. Everything looked okay until May 2005 when Chappelle stunned the world by unexpectedly quitting the show in mid-production and fleeing to South Africa where he would remain for the next two weeks, amid rumors that he had become an inmate in a mental health facility.

In the ensuing standoff, the network demanded Chappelle's return to the production set while the comedian vowed never to return unless big changes were made to his working conditions. As a condition for his possible return, Chappelle requested that the network not air the unfinished material prepared for the show's third season, stuff that he hated.

In the end, neither side got what it wanted: Chappelle went back to doing live stand-up comedy and never returned to Comedy Central; for its part, Comedy Central ignored Chappelle's wish by airing the unfinished material from the comedian's abandoned third season around July of that year (the so-called Lost Episodes) plus an uncensored DVD of the disputed material.

The disappointment on both sides is no surprise. For starters, this was a contract for "personal services" and courts normally would not force an unwilling person to render a personal service to another person. The simple reason here is that there is no way for the courts to ensure that one person serves another in good faith and properly: the courts are not job supervisors. So, Chappelle didn't have to return to work. Yet, if it would have had a provision such as a negative covenant in its contract with Chappelle, Comedy Central could use an injunction from the court to prevent Chappelle from working for a rival TV network during the time he was supposed to be working for Comedy Central.

The core issue here is creative differences, as Neal Brennan, the co-creator of the show, correctly observed. Chappelle simply didn't think he had his creative space: he said he felt awful every day he worked on the show and felt like some kind of prostitute. "I want to be well-rounded, and the industry is a place of extremes," he famously said. Apparently, Comedy Central did not see things the same way.

The big lesson here for comedians is that, in an industry "of extremes," they must look out for themselves right from the time the contract is being negotiated. The good news is, we have freedom of contract in America and, in most cases, folks can put in pretty much any clauses they want in their contracts. Comedians must pay close attention to clauses in the agreement that pertain to creative space and format for the shows.

And this is important because what is good for the bottom line of the TV networks may not necessarily be good for the comedian's career and emotional well-being.

For instance, Chappelle reportedly said he did not personally like the sketch-comedy format. Yet that was exactly what his contract with Comedy Central required him to do on the show. And he went along with it until the so-called "pixie sketch" on the show freaked him out when he reportedly discovered somebody laughing at him instead of laughing with him. Well, today, he's moved back to doing his favored stand-up comedy.

A final word: A blockbuster deal with a major TV network that employs a lot of lawyers can often seem like getting in a gun fight, and no comedian should go into that gun fight with just a knife. So, just be ready to negotiate hard and don't forget to "lawyer up"!

CONAN'S NBC: No Laughing Matter for a Funnyman

California
January 24, 2010

On Sunday, January 10, 2010, NBC made it official that it would cancel the 10 p.m. *Jay Leno Show* and move Leno over to an 11:35 p.m. time slot. NBC offered Conan O'Brien, the funnyman from Harvard, the chance to move his *Tonight Show* back just a half hour from 11:35 p.m. to 12:05 a.m., to be followed by Jimmy Fallon's *Late Show*.

Looking back now, the Leno-O'Brien shuffle by NBC Universal's boss Jeff Zucker easily looks "boneheaded" because, with Leno gone, Letterman now rules the ratings at 11:35 p.m. in spite of O'Brien's best efforts. Plus, Leno himself is doing rather poorly at 10.p.m., as NBC languishes in fourth place among the major networks. This is now being called Late Night Crisis 2010. Disaster all around!

Yet, NBC won't be getting its wish: O'Brien is leaving in a foul mood with an unfriendly dig at NBC, which he accuses of making him a scapegoat for its "terrible" prime time ratings. He also claims that starting the *Tonight Show* at 12:05 a.m. the next day amounts to a "destruction" of the show. O'Brien's bold reaction somehow recalls an earlier and bigger drama on the *Tonight Show* when Jack Paar stormed off the show in 1960 to protest alleged censorship from NBC folks.

When the dust settles, O'Brien will leave NBC with millions of dollars in his pocket. But some people have wondered what the scenario could have looked like if the funnyman had chosen to stay and fight instead. No easy answers here, but there are options all around the table.

Speaking of O'Brien's options, a small oversight by his lawyers may have made all the difference against him, something that NBC has to be thankful for. And here it is: the language of the agreement did not include that O'Brien's *Tonight Show* must be held at 11:35 p.m. And NBC has ended up using this oversight as an escape route. Recall that NBC told O'Brien he could carry his show intact over to 12:05 a.m.

If that loophole didn't exist, O'Brien's legs would be stronger in a fight against NBC if he had chosen to stick around and mix it up with them. He could easily seek an "injunction" from a court to prevent NBC from moving Leno to 11:35 p.m. Plus, he could also request an order of "specific performance" to make NBC keep its word to leave him on at 11:35 p.m. Not having these options made O'Brien something of a sitting duck as NBC selfishly maneuvered to fix Zucker's big blunder earlier on, in moving Leno into the 10 p.m. slot. Some have described NBC's tactic against O'Brien as "Machiavellian."

To be sure, O'Brien isn't the only one with options here. His contract with NBC reportedly contains what's called a "negative covenant" that could allow NBC to keep him off any rival television networks during the time he was supposed to be working for NBC. Already, Zucker is said to be "threatening to ice him" if he walks away from NBC. All this is important because FOX is reportedly interested in hiring O'Brien to launch Fox's own rival late night show.

But, aside from Fox's interest in O'Brien, can NBC really enforce any agreement to keep O'Brien off late night television for even one day? Not likely, under the circumstances.

For starters, NBC has not dealt fairly and in good faith with O'Brien, and the law requires a party complaining to come with "clean hands." Plus, the courts would probably find such an action "unreasonable" since the law aims to protect both competition in the marketplace as well as a person's right to earn a living. So, one can safely predict that if push comes to shove here, NBC will likely suffer the same fate that ABC endured in 1980 when ABC failed in its suit against CBS in trying to stop sportscaster Warner Wolf from jumping ship to CBS.

True, O'Brien has asked us not to "feel sorry" for him and, considering all the big money he's leaving with (about $30 million by some estimates), perhaps we shouldn't. Yet we cannot help but wonder just what could have been had the Ivy League funnyman been in a good position to really take the fight to NBC.

HOWARD STERN vs. SIRIUS XM: Starting a Fire in the House

New York
June 3, 2011

Howard Stern is a major newsmaker with a large footprint, and these days he is starting some fires inside the house of Sirius XM satellite radio.

This past March, the humorist and self-styled "king of all media" sued Sirius XM [through his production company, One Twelve Inc.,] in a Manhattan court alleging breach of contract against the satellite radio company for unpaid stock awards under their contract. Also suing Sirius XM is Don Buchwald, the agent for One Twelve, Inc., who is claiming a consultation fee allegedly promised him under the agreement.

And it all comes down to what the agreement said or did not say about what happens if and when the big bucks start rolling in. Stern says the agreement requires Sirius to compensate him in the form of additional company stock every time his presence causes the number of subscribers to Sirius XM to increase over a certain number set in advance throughout the five-year period. Sirius XM begs to differ and claims that it has met all its "obligations under the terms of our [the] 2004 agreement with Howard, his agent and production company." Sirius XM also says it is "surprised and disappointed" by the lawsuit, which means that it has no plans to pony up to Stern and his agent any time soon.

It may seem rather odd that the parties continue to do business together despite the lawsuit, but this shouldn't be too surprising given that the collaboration has been very lucrative for both parties so far. What's not to like about smiling to the bank. (In January 2011, Stern got another five years on his contract for an estimated

$400 million and Sirius XM is now twenty million subscribers stronger.)

It is interesting that Stern did not raise this issue of the additional stock awards until during the last year of the contract. So, can he now turn around and seek to enforce the right he seemed to have abandoned for years? Or does his silence over those years somehow mean that perhaps he knew he didn't have the right he is now trying to enforce? Could this be some Monday morning quarterbacking to corral more money? Stern claims that he held back out of sympathy for Sirius' financial situation following its acquisition of rival XM in 2008. Yeah, right, one might well say. This obviously seems like a lame explanation in the all-too practical world of businesspeople. As that famous saying goes (in English company law), "Charity has no business sitting on the board of directors." And everyone knows that Stern is a business-savvy guy.

And there is the issue of the Sirius/XM merger. Assuming that the agreement in fact requires payment by additional stock awards to Stern, does the number of subscribers include the people coming in from the XM side of the ledger? Or is it limited to just the folks from the old Sirius alone? In talking about compensation based on performance or "rainmaking," it may not be easy to just put them all in the same pot, especially if the XM subscribers were brought in simply because of the merger, and not directly because of anything Stern did. Take this loose analogy: If someone promised you $1 million if you have five children in ten years, can you still claim that money on the same footing in ten years if some of the five kids you are presenting happen to be adopted? This may be debatable.

However, one thing is for sure: if Stern is in fact entitled to get what he is claiming, then that particular clause in the agreement was so poorly drafted that it did him no favors at all. He shouldn't have needed to go to court in order to receive what should be rightfully his. It all comes back to the old lesson among lawyers that a badly drafted agreement usually hands off an unnecessary lawsuit to the lawyer's client and would often only help the person who is under obligation to do something for the benefit of the other person. In this case, it would be Sirius XM.

Still, just because Sirius XM may well be ahead on points doesn't mean it would welcome this kind of publicity, especially coming from a media sensation with a big microphone like Howard Stern (who is remarkable for his on-air remarks when talking with the callers on his show). So far, he's kept a surprisingly low profile on the whole thing, but who knows for how long. Also, the lawsuit itself is simply not good for business, to say the least: the day after it was filed, the company's shares fell off a bit and some analysts downgraded them from Buy to Hold. Translation: these circumstances may be good grounds for Sirius XM to consider settling the case just to put out the in-house fires. And keep the courts out of the company's business.

CASE UPDATE: While the outbreak of the lawsuit itself was a surprise to many, the actual end result wasn't that surprising. On April 11, 2013, the court dismissed Howard Stern's case against Sirius XM Radio. The court flat out said that the parties' contract was "unambiguous" and that since the additional subscribers to Sirius XM's operations came from the XM Radio side of the ledger, Stern's deal did not give him a claim to any monies from those sources.

Sound familiar? You may recall the so-called loose analogy I made earlier in the original discussion of the case above, which went something like this: "If someone promised you $1 million if you have five children in ten years, can you still claim that money on the same footing in ten years if some of the five kids you are presenting happen to be adopted? Well, obviously, the New York appeals court didn't think so. If Stern really wanted it to be so, then he should have used more "unambiguous" language in his contract.

ADAM CAROLLA: Juggling Comedy, Business and Friendship in Court

California
June 9, 2013

Funnyman Adam Carolla has quite a situation on his hands these days. And he does have some court dates coming up where he'll be sorting out a few money matters with some old friends. It all comes back to the whole idea that doing business with other folks is never an easy thing and there is no guarantee that things would get any easier just because those other folks happen to be a guy's close pals. Especially when business starts to boom, and it comes time to divvy up the money. But first, here's the story.

Around February 2009, Carolla's radio gig, *The Adam Carolla Show*, was unexpectedly canceled by CBS. That was when Donny Misraje, a longtime close friend of Carolla's suggested that the comedian roll his show over to a daily podcast as a way to "retain his avid fan base."

According to Misraje, he and Carolla agreed to form a partnership business to pursue the new venture together. Under the oral agreement, Carolla was to hold a sixty percent interest in the partnership, leaving thirty percent to Misraje and his wife Kathee, and another ten percent to a guy named Sandy Ganz.

Misraje claimed that by 2011 profits from the business had grown by a lot and that Carolla had begun shutting out all three of the other stakeholders from the operations of the business, including at one point, banning him (the producer) from being on site at the live show. He said that by the end of October 2011, Carolla had fired all three of them altogether and was refusing to honor the partnership agreement. In response, Misraje and his co-plaintiffs filed a lawsuit against Carolla, alleging breach of the partnership agreement plus a demand for accounting, and the imposition of a constructive trust for their benefit and protection; and more.

21

The outcome of this case could provide some clarity for the benefit of the many comedians on the late-night TV shows, radio shows, podcasts, and comedy specials who work under various arrangements, promises and understandings with their buddies, whether as show sidekicks, as producers, or as whatever else they're asked to do on the shows.

The starting point in figuring out this case is to determine if there was indeed a partnership agreement between the parties, and if so, whether Carolla's actions violated the terms of that partnership. If the answer is yes, then the next thing is to figure out what kind of remedy can be awarded in order to set things right.

Under the law, a partnership relationship arises when two or more people carry on business together for profit. And the agreement between any two or more people to form a partnership could either be written down in a document somewhere or it could be made orally as by word of mouth. Regardless of whether the agreement was written or oral, what must exist in every case is that each partner had the "intent" to enter into the partnership with the other partners, and that each of them "consented" to become partners with one another. In short, the partners must be on the same page as to whether they want to form a partnership. Business lawyers often refer to this requirement as a "meeting of the minds" between the folks involved. And this requirement is a pretty big deal because in the eyes of the law, each partner is an "agent" of the other partners, and his actions could bind the other partners whether they like it or not. Also, the partners are considered "co-owners" of the business, meaning that all the partners have the right to participate in the management of the business and the sharing of its profits.

Therefore, as in every partnership case, the simple question here is whether Carolla intended to and consented to become partners with Misraje and the others. In other words, was there a "meeting of the minds" between Carolla and the plaintiffs to form a partnership? Well, since we do not have a written agreement here, the intention and consent of the parties to become partners will have to be gathered from their actions at the time that their collaboration began, as well as the period before and after. These actions are usually referred to as "course of conduct" and they are deemed to shed light on what the parties had in mind when they were interacting with one another.

Speaking of "course of conduct" between the parties, the courts have over the years come up with certain ways of reading between the lines when attempting to figure out the intentions of folks involved in contract situations. And the process can sometimes be tricky because this surely isn't a perfect science. Usually, when the evidence presented by both sides is sort of evenly balanced and could go either way, the courts come down in favor of the person who is denying that there is a partnership.

Here's how it works: In one case that happened in New York, the first guy claimed that he gave a certain amount of money to the other guy in exchange for a ten percent partnership stake in a restaurant business. (Both guys had been close pals for over twenty years at the time.) However, the other guy claimed that the money was a "loan" rather than a "capital investment" in the restaurant business. It was shown that the first guy who lived in Washington, DC, visited the restaurant just once or twice during the first year that it opened; that he gave out menus and business cards about the restaurant to other folks; and that he requested a friend of his in the media to feature the restaurant in a prominent magazine. The court concluded that these actions could have been the actions of a guy just trying to help his friend's business rather than the actions of a person acting as a partner in a business. The court instead gave more weight to all the things (get this!) that he did not do. For instance, that he did not inquire about the leases; the contracts; the insurance; and the debts of the business. Also, he did not raise or discuss with his supposed partner any concerns about the profits or losses of the business; nor did he indicate in any of his loan applications or tax returns filed during that time period that he had acquired a partnership interest in the restaurant.

In the Carolla case, it is interesting that Misraje has taken pains in his Complaint to outline actions and steps that he and the other plaintiffs took to establish the intention and consent of all the parties to the partnership, including Carolla. As consideration for his stake in the business, Misraje (an experienced producer and editor) claims that he was to produce and manage the show. He also claims that he quit his entertainment industry job paying $231,000 annually in order to focus on his work at Carolla's podcast, which carried no salary at all. During this time, he claimed that he and his family lived off a home equity line of credit on their property. In addition, Misraje said he kicked in $10,000 worth of personal equipment and supplies into the business operations of the podcast plus other sacrifices that he and his wife made. For his part, Carolla was to be the star of the comedy show, while Ganz would contribute his expertise in technology as consideration for his own share of the business. Obviously, if Misraje's side can sustain these claims in court, they'll likely have a far better day in court than the restaurant guy described above.

Of course, if the court finds that there is no partnership relationship between the parties, then it is game over for the plaintiffs, meaning that Carolla wins. However, if the court finds that there is in fact a partnership situation between them, then the action next shifts to the question of "remedies," where the court decides how to set matters right between the parties. And the courts can be pretty flexible when they are dealing with the issue of remedies. For starters, considering that each partner is entitled to participate both in management and profit sharing, for one partner to exclude a fellow partner from the operations of the business or to refuse to share profits with another partner is a violation of the partnership relationship, and such an action would be a good cause to dissolve the partnership. In real life, what usually happens when partners can't agree on the way forward is that the court will "order" the partners not to shut out one another from the business and will appoint a "receiver" to run the affairs of the business until the court proceedings are finished.

However, appointing a receiver may be more appropriate to situations where partners are, for instance, running a restaurant than where they are running a podcast show. Unlike a restaurant and similar businesses, life in the entertainment world tends to be quite personal in nature and the show itself (including the buzz and the ratings) is all about the "star" of the show. Therefore, as a practical matter, it will be unusual and pretty messy for the court, for instance, to order Carolla to allow Misraje to keep producing his show against his will. Plus, since receivers are folks who take over the business operations in the meantime from the partners, a receiver just won't work in this particular situation since Carolla, as the star of the show, will still be front and center of the show. (The show simply cannot go on without him.) Long story short, receivers and injunctions just won't cut it in this case.

However, that doesn't mean it's the end of the case. What will likely happen is that the court (if it finds that a "partnership" exists) will impose a 'constructive trust' upon Carolla for the benefit of the other partners. In this case, the thing being held in 'trust' by Carolla will be the share of the profits and other assets of the partnership that rightfully belong to Misraje and the other co-owners. (A "constructive trust" situation arises when someone is deemed to be holding something for the benefit of another person and it usually arises when the courts want to prevent "unjust enrichment" of one person at the expense of another in the interest of justice.) And with constructive trusts comes an obligation to render "accounting" and to distribute the stuff that's being held in trust.

In the end, this case has the makings of a horse race. And because the burden is on his opponents to prove that it was in fact a partnership arrangement that they had with him, rather than something else, the slight advantage is with Carolla at the early going. Yet, Misraje's side clearly looks like they've come ready to play and, for sure, they've put a lot on the table so far. If the case is not ultimately settled, it's tough to say just how the decision will come down. Regardless of how it ends, though, it is pretty likely that the result of this case will be of genuine interest to folks in the comedy industry at large.

CASE UPDATE: The case between the former high school pals went to trial in fall 2014 in a Los Angeles Superior Court, and just one week in, it was all over. On September 9, 2014, after Carolla had been cross examined by the plaintiffs' (Misrajes') lawyer, the parties announced a settlement that same day in a surprising termination of the litigation. The terms of the mid-trial settlement were not disclosed. Earlier that May, the court had refused Carolla's request to end the litigation and had ruled instead that the case should proceed to trial. The reason the court gave was that Misraje had presented evidence to show that "Carolla often referred to his relationship with Misraje as a partnership . . . and that plaintiffs shared in partnership profits, contributed to the partnership, and helped to manage the partnership."

CHARLIE SHEEN SUES WARNER BROS. "BIG" TIME:
Who's Winning Yet?

California
April 2, 2011

Last month, the Charlie Sheen saga entered a major new phase when the Hollywood studio Warner Bros. fired him from the hit CBS sitcom *Two and a Half Men*. At the time he was fired, Sheen was yet to complete about eight episodes in the 24-episode schedule of his latest contract signed in May last year.

A few days after his dismissal from the show, Sheen made good on his vow to sue them "big." And sue them "big" he did, both for himself and the show's out-of-work crew. Sheen hit Warner Bros. and the show's producer Chuck Lorre with a breach of contract claim for more than $100 million dollars for halting production of the comedy show. The suit also tagged on a claim for punitive damages. Sheen claims he is entitled to be fully paid on his contract whether or not he completed the 24 episodes of the show that his contract required.

So, does Sheen really have the right to get paid for the remaining episodes that he did not work on? Well, so far, the legal experts out there are not answering this question with one voice. But here's how it looks.

To win his breach of contract action, Sheen will need to show that his contract was valid and that he was able and ready to do his part. Whenever they happen, "punitive damages" are the courts' way of telling the public not to follow the bad example of the person being punished with the damages.

Warner Bros. claims that it fired Sheen for several reasons, which together add up to Sheen being "unable to perform the essential duties of his position." The studio listed stuff like Sheen having trouble remembering his lines; Sheen missing his rehearsals and sometimes showing up for work with little or no sleep and therefore needing to lean on furniture to maintain his balance. And then there was Sheen's public behavior and rants against Lorre, which the studio considered as "inflammatory comments poisoning key working relationships."

Since Sheen's contract as an actor is a contract for "personal services," these on-the-job allegations made against him, if true, would mean that Sheen's actions deprived Warner Bros. of the benefits it expected from his contract and would, therefore, provide the studio with a good defense to Sheen's lawsuit. Because, unlike a contract for the sale of goods, where you could perhaps "cover" or replace a nonperforming TV set or car with another one, personal service contracts for artists are regarded as "unique" and therefore faithful "performance" of the job by the actor or musician under contract is a must-have. Nothing less will do.

Yet the devil is in the details, and Warner Bros.' case is not looking exactly easy. First, Sheen claims he attempted to return to the series in mid-February but was told that Lorre had not prepared production scripts for the season's remaining episodes. If true, it would mean that Sheen showed up ready and willing to work but the studio was not.

If this were a scoring game, Sheen would be ahead on points, as long as we are talking about the "remaining episodes" of the show. For starters, most of the studio's allegations against him are things he did on the show in the past, which the studio itself may already have "acquiesced" in or gone along with since 2003 when the show started its run. Besides, despite Sheen's alleged (mis)conduct, the show always appeared on TV on its regular schedule and Sheen always appeared to TV audiences to be fine in the role he was playing; and the show remained the highest rated TV sitcom regardless.

Plus, Warner Bros.' recent gripes about Sheen's behavior seem a little like Monday morning quarterbacking. For instance, while it was allegedly happening, the studio didn't suspend him from the show or dock any one of his reported $1.8 million paychecks.

Nor was the studio unable to run any episode of the show on its regular schedule because of Sheen's misconduct. Indeed, some commentators have even suggested that the studio wrote scenes in a number of the episodes to reflect Sheen's real life bad-boy behavior.

If Warner Bros. wanted to fire him without headaches, they went about the whole business the wrong way, it seems. Given Sheen's history of bad behavior in the past and his recent embarrassing public behavior and shocking rants against Lorre, Sheen was something of a disaster waiting to happen anyway, at least before the remaining episodes were done. But it looks like Warner Bros. did not have the patience to wait for Sheen to cross the red lines before firing him. They moved too quickly. (Talk about cops arresting a guy just because they believe he'll beat up his girlfriend any day now. Wrong!)

Perhaps, the case will settle out of court or in arbitration. Otherwise, the odds are running in Sheen's favor, and though he may not get all the money he thinks he's entitled to receive (or for that matter, any punitive damages at all), Warner Bros. will likely end up paying him well. But at least, Warner Bros. will have the satisfaction of getting the pesky Sheen out of their system.

CASE UPDATE: Charlie Sheen's $100 million dollar lawsuit lasted for about six months.

On September 26, 2011, Warner Bros Television released the following statement: "Warner Bros. Television, Chuck Lorre and Charlie Sheen have resolved their dispute to the parties' mutual satisfaction. The pending lawsuit and arbitration will be dismissed as to all parties. The parties have agreed to maintain confidentiality over the terms of the settlement."

However, it was reported by online news site *The Wrap* that in order to get Sheen to walk away the studio shelled out $25 million, with promises of more money from syndication revenues.

JON LOVITZ: Taking the "Business" of Comedy to the Courthouse

California
May 11, 2013

With comedy as big as it is these days, there is no better time than now for anyone on the business side of the industry to make a ton of money, especially those who know the industry pretty well— or should. Folks like comedian Jon Lovitz. Needless to say, when rough times hit, the gravy train can also simply get derailed and spill a lot of money down the drain. Sometimes, a lot of money, as Lovitz, a former *Saturday Night Live* star, claimed in his lawsuit against the former manager of his comedy club. Here's what happened.

In 2009, Lovitz went into the comedy club business with a partner named Frank Kelley. Together, they set up the Jon Lovitz Comedy Club in Universal City, California, with Kelley acting as the manager of the club. A few years later, after losing a lot of money, the business eventually failed. Then the blame game erupted. Typical scenario! Lovitz claims he had invested more than $1.5 million dollars in the failed business, and he blames Kelley for running the business into the ground. He also accuses Kelley of embezzling at least $100,000 of the club's money. Lovitz is mad as hell. Not letting matters slide, Lovitz filed a lawsuit against Kelley seeking huge money damages from the former manager for fraud, conversion, and breach of fiduciary duty.

Lovitz' lawsuit is one of those situations where someone might wonder why the district attorney's office isn't involved at all, considering all the fraud allegations that seem to suggest a pattern of criminal behavior on the part of Kelley, including the allegation that Kelley falsified books and accounts. Well, the short answer for those who might be wondering about this situation is that much of these events occurred among business partners in the running of their business, and the DA's offices usually have bigger fishes to fry in chasing down violent criminals or more serious financial crimes rather than spending taxpayers' money on some garden-variety accusations of betrayals among business partners and associates.

Such cases are usually left to the civil courts and so Lovitz' case is taking place in just the proper venue. Yet the Lovitz case is important in today's comedy industry where comedy clubs are on the rise again after declining in the 1990s. The outcome of this case would at least help both comedy club managers and the club owners who hire them to run the clubs to know, for example, where the lines are drawn in their relationship with each other as well as the circumstances in which club managers can get in trouble for the way they're doing their jobs.

But can Lovitz win his claims based on fraud, conversion, or breach of fiduciary duty? Well, let's look at the law. For starters, this is a case about business partners who trusted each other so much that one partner literally handed the keys to the lock box to the other partner in hopes he would run their common enterprise honestly and profitably. In such a situation, the "trusted" guy running the business owes more than just a "thank you" to the guy who's coming up with the money. Folks like the guy running the business are regarded in law as "fiduciaries" of the other person. The law imposes the status of fiduciary in most transactions where there is a relationship of "trust and confidence" existing between two people. Typically, in such situations, one person often knows so much about what's going on in the transaction and is so much in control of the situation that unless the confidence and trust is maintained, the other person who is thus placed in a weaker position could get hurt.

So, in order to protect the other person involved, the law obliges the "fiduciary" to act in a trustworthy and transparent manner. One of the biggest requirements imposed upon a fiduciary is that he not put himself in any position where there is a conflict of interest between himself and his duties. In short, a fiduciary is not allowed to benefit himself either at the expense of the work he is hired to do or that of the person who hired him or her to do the work. Aside from business managers, the typical situations where we'll find fiduciary relationships are the situations like those between a lawyer and his or her client or a doctor and his or her patient.

Considering what being a fiduciary is all about, there is little doubt that Kelley's work as a fiduciary of Lovitz is the issue that dominates all others in this case. All the other claims in this case are not nearly as important as the question of whether Kelley's actions amount to a violation of his fiduciary duties of good faith and fair dealing with Lovitz in the way he handled the affairs of the club. (By the way, given the actual claims that Lovitz is making in this case, some of the allegations in his lawsuit seem sort of idle and unnecessary. For example, since Lovitz is not trying to cancel or "rescind" the agreement on the basis of "fraud in the inducement," all the talk about Kelley hyping his qualifications and track record as a comedy club manager in the Los Angeles area just to get Lovitz to hire him as club manager aren't really helpful in supporting any claim stated in the lawsuit. To be sure, this case is well past the "rescission" stage at this time.)

But seriously, how will the court proceed to sort out the actual claims that have been made in the case? As already noted, all the above claims are closely related and ultimately revolve around the whole question of Kelley being a fiduciary. In layman's language, the claim about fraud is really sort of like saying that somebody's actions were deceitful (or dishonest) and misleading, and that they caused a detriment or disadvantage to somebody else. With respect to "conversion," we're talking about the actions of someone who treats another person's property as if the said property instead belonged to him and in so doing deprived the true owner of the property of the benefit and use of that property. Typically, this occurs in 'bailment' situations where one person entrusts property to the custody of another person on a temporary basis. The claim of breach of fiduciary duty, as explained above, means that someone in a position of trust and confidence betrayed the trust placed in him by another person by taking unfair advantage of their position to the disadvantage of the other person. Of course, in each situation involved in these claims, the plaintiffs must allege that they suffered damage or loss as a result of the defendants' actions. Without the damage factor, there will be no liability.

For someone trying to win money damages for his former partner's breach of fiduciary duty, it sure looks like Lovitz is playing a winning hand with the kinds of allegations he has made in his lawsuit. For instance, he claims that Kelley used the comedy club's checks and credit cards to pay for his own personal expenses, and that in so doing he failed or neglected to use the club's monies to meet the club's obligations, such as paying both performers who did gigs at the club as well as the club's own staffers. The allegations that someone in a fiduciary position like Kelley has used the assets of the business as his own "piggy bank" and that he re-routed the company's assets to his own personal benefit and use lie at the heart of a case based on the breach of fiduciary duty. Lovitz claims that Kelley swiped more than $100,000 in credit card expenses for which the club was ultimately held responsible.

Yet as good as the allegations are, that's not the end of the matter. Not even close. For one thing, this is only one side of the story and surely the devil is in the details with this one: making the allegations is the easy part, proving the allegations is the real heavy lifting here. In this case, Lovitz will likely need to prove that the expenses Kelley ran up had nothing at all to do with the business. It won't be enough to show that he spent too much money on certain things or that he spent money on the wrong things. Or even that his failure to spend money on some things or in certain ways led to the failure of the business. That just won't cut it in this kind of case, especially because people who manage stuff are allowed the discretion to choose their ways and means of operation. (In other contexts, they call this sort of idea the "business judgment rule.")

When there's some doubt here, they will often award the benefit of the doubt to the guy making the business decision. So, in terms of his liability, it all pretty much comes down to whether Kelley intended to act in violation of his fiduciary duty, or whether he was simply being a bad manager. In other words, was Kelley acting on purpose to rip off the business operation, or was he just being a sloppy manager? To be sure, answering these kinds of questions aren't the easiest things to do in the 'cloud and dust' of a full-dress courtroom trial. And, as one might predict, defense lawyers more than plaintiffs' lawyers simply enjoy the uncertainty of these answers.

In the end, running a comedy club, just like any business, isn't easy, and winning a case like this one isn't easy either. From all indications, a lot of money has apparently gone down the drain here, and what we have is a bad case of misplaced trust and confidence in the hiring of a business manager. Needless to say, it was Lovitz' job to hire a good manager for his business. Yet one can't help but notice that it is in this particular context that Lovitz' allegations of being misled about Kelley's qualifications and background seem to make the most sense. The larger point here, though, is that as far as we're dealing with financial loss or damage resulting from the actions of a business manager or decisions made by him, this kind of problem generally couldn't have been prevented by a written contract or agreement, no matter how smartly crafted. Fact is, there is only so much anyone can write into an agreement today to control the turbulent waters of human events tomorrow, especially the uncertainties of the business world.

It is hard to predict the outcome of a case like this one and it would be interesting to see how it all shakes out in court, assuming of course that an out-of-court settlement isn't hammered out between the parties.

Yet, however it all winds down, for a guy like funnyman Lovitz, who apparently has lost a lot of money, this whole situation surely is no laughing matter.

CASE UPDATE: On November 19, 2014, a joint statement was released by the parties' lawyers announcing that the former partners had "amicably resolved" their differences and have mutually dismissed the case. Case settled.

CONTROVERSY AT EDINBURGH FRINGE: The Right to Perform at a Comedy Venue

Britain
June 8, 2012

Competition breeds tension, and as more people than ever flock to comedy venues to catch some laughs, tensions are rising in the backrooms as the folks who run the comedy shows try to outdo one another in the race for audience members. And as the turf wars heat up, pushing the boundaries is just something that goes with the territory: Not long ago, the Edinburgh Free Fringe Festival (also called the PBH Free Fringe) reportedly changed its rules in a way that prevents any comic performing at any of its venues from performing at any venue that is run by the Laughing Horse, a rival organizer of free festivals.

One fallout of the new rule was that a certain comedian who had been booked for a later gig at an Edinburgh Free Fringe event was forced to pull out of an earlier variety show (*Greatest Show on Legs*) slated for The Hive, a Laughing Horse venue. For American comedians this would be sort of like the New York Comedy Festival telling its comedians that they cannot perform at, say, the South Beach Comedy Festival.

Commentators and other observers of the comedy scene have knocked the move by PBH Free Fringe as a "restriction of trade" that is damaging to the careers of up-and-coming comics. (By the way, if the commentators were lawyers, they'd probably be calling the practice at PBH by its legal jargon, which is "restraint of trade.")

To be sure, these tensions are a fact of life in the real world: First, a comedian who is pretty good at his game and is in high demand can have, say, a stand-up gig in one venue and yet another stand-up gig or even a spot on a sketch show at a separate venue altogether. Yet we live in a free-market society where promoters of comedy events or owners of venues for comedy and variety shows have the power to set whatever "rules of the game" they can get away with for the participants in their shows and, of course, they can charge whatever fees they want at their venues.

But there is no doubt the rules at PBH Free Fringe (Edinburgh) will create a new and different field of play for comedians working in that circuit. At the minimum, it will restrict the ability or freedom of comedians to perform wherever they can get a gig or wherever they'd like to perform. But then again, is the new rule at PBH Free Fringe something that amounts to "restraint of trade," as in the kind of behavior that the law frowns upon and does not allow? Does it cross the big red line? Well, let's open the law book.

By the way, in the PBH case, the performer did not give us the chance to find out the answer to this question as he ducked the confrontation with the festival organizers by dropping out of the Laughing Horse event at The Hive. It sure would have been a more interesting and perhaps, fun scenario if he would have chosen instead to stand his ground and fight. But he didn't.

Anyhow, for starters, the principle of "restraint of trade" sets out to protect the rights of folks out there to practice their profession or trade by cutting off any attempts by other folks to interfere with that right. The typical situation where the issue of restraint of trade comes up is where an employer signs an employment contract with an employee and the contract requires the employee not to set up a competing business after he leaves the employer's job either because he quits or is fired. Restraint of trade could also become an issue between, say, a new comedy club owner and the person from whom he is acquiring the comedy club business.

In these two situations above, the obvious goal of the former employer in the first situation and the new comedy club owner in the second is to prevent the employee and the former club owner, respectively, from setting up a rival business to compete against them in the same line of business in the same area or district. Usually, these agreements set out the length of time during which the other person cannot set up a rival business, as well as the geographical area where he cannot set up a rival business. These deals are called "non-compete agreements" and usually they will be rejected by the courts if the courts find them to be "unreasonable." The whole talk about the restriction being unreasonable is just a shorthand way of saying that the restriction imposed on the other person is simply too "overreaching" to be tolerated, either because of the public interest or because it is flat out unfair to the other person.

What qualifies as "unreasonable" depends on the circumstances of each case, but the simple rule of thumb is this: If the restriction reaches further than it needs to go (either because it is too long in terms of period of time during which the restriction is in effect, or because it is too wide in terms of geographical area or space covered by the restriction), then it probably is unreasonable and will be rejected by the courts. To say, for instance, that a former employee cannot work in the same city where a former employer has his place of business, say New York City, isn't likely to pass the test of reasonableness for the simple reason that it is just too wide in terms of space. The bottom line here is that as long as he maintains a "reasonable" distance from the former employer's place of business, the former employee must be allowed to work and earn his living without undue interference.

Speaking of comedians who deal with event organizers or owners of comedy venues, one thing is sort of clear: it is not that easy for them to bring themselves under the protection of the restraint of trade principle. For starters, when most comedians work at these venues, usually they just go in there, take care of their gigs, and they're done. They often don't stick around to take on the status of "employees" at the comedy clubs or venues where they do gigs. Plus, many times, most comedians who do gigs at these venues do not have the cookie cutter written contracts that come with all the bells and whistles of a typical employment contract between a hospital and a doctor who works at the facility, for instance. Comedians just live in a different world than that.

So, the situation at PBH Free Fringe (or Edinburgh Fringe) will obviously curtail the freedom of comics to do as many gigs as they can or should be able to do. And probably the commentators are also right to get pissed off and talk about things like "restriction of trade" in the layman's parlance. But as a practical matter, the situation with the new rule at the PBH Fringe isn't exactly the kind of situation where the legal principle of "restraint of trade" will be too helpful to any comedians who might wish to fight the PBH rules. That situation, perhaps unfortunately, belongs in the free market scenario of "take-it-or-leave it," a place where life isn't always fair, and folks are told in effect to change the TV channel if they don't like the show they're watching.

But there are situations where the principle of "restraint of trade" could come in handy for comedians and the work they do. Take a situation where a veteran comedian is under contract with a comedy club to run a New Talent Show for the club (in places like New York, these shows are also called "bringers"). Usually, such veteran comedians would be considered as "independent contractors" and may be allowed to do other work on the side, such as running a comedy school either at the club itself or even at a separate location. While the New Talent show directors are working on the inside at a particular comedy club, they often are able to acquire important information or even business secrets that might be useful to somebody else competing against the said club. In such situations, the comedy club or comedy venue where they are working might be justified in trying to use a "non-compete agreement" to prevent them from running the same kind of shows for a rival club. If the said veteran comedian tries to work for a rival comedy club, then his former club can go get a court order (or injunction) to stop him from doing so. Of course, whether the former comedy club will be successful in preventing him from working for a cross town rival club will depend on whether or not the former club can convince the courts that the terms of such restriction are "reasonable." If the restriction "overreaches," it will be tossed out.

Also, if a comedian signs on as a "resident" comedian with a comedy club or comedy venue and gets paid regularly the same way as any other employee, such as a bartender who works at the place, then of course, a non-compete agreement would apply to such a comedian as well, meaning that the comedy club can then try to stop him from working for a rival club in that same capacity.

In the end the controversial new rule at the Edinburgh's PBH Free Fringe is only the latest tactic in the cutthroat competition that is gripping the comedy industry today, as more and more people join the comedy bandwagon at various venues. And it certainly won't be the last time that a competitor comes up with a new tactic in the escalating turf wars in the backrooms of comedy.

"COMICS UNLEASHED": A Money Tangle in the Courtroom

California
February 9, 2013

Comics Unleashed Productions is living up to its name these days in the courtroom thanks to some comedians who have trouble with the way it does business. The production company is one of the entities under the umbrella of comedian Byron Allen's company Entertainment Studios (ES), which produces shows for syndication and digital distribution. And from the look of things both sides have a fair amount of stuff to sort out before this thing blows over.

In December 2013, in Los Angeles Superior Court, two former employees of the company filed a class action lawsuit against Allen himself, Entertainment Studios, and business entities affiliated with them, alleging breach of contract, unfair business practices, and failure to pay wages that were due to them. The plaintiffs, Bernadette Pauley, and Thomas Clark, both comedians, claimed that they performed work on the syndicated show *Comics.TV* under a contract with Comics Unleashed Productions and were not paid for their work. The plaintiffs also claim that they were owed "residuals" as well as reimbursement for work-related expenses.

Before talking about the plaintiffs' chances of winning the lawsuit, the first question is whether this case can even survive as a class action. The typical class action lawsuit usually involves folks who have been injured in a similar or common fashion by a similar or common cause and are seeking a similar or common remedy. One good example here would be the case of folks who have been injured by a bad product manufactured by a company, such as a "defective" drug. Or perhaps folks who have been injured in an accident owing to a "defective" gas pedal in an automobile.

However, this situation was not your typical class action scenario: Pauley claimed in the lawsuit that she hosted about four episodes

41

of *Comics.TV* and that Clark appeared as a stand-up comedian in at least one of the episodes of the show. In all, the lawsuit claims that there are about 112 comics and actors who worked on various episodes of the show. It's also safe to assume that these plaintiffs are asking for different kinds of payments from Allen's side: for example, each person on the plaintiffs' side likely has a different basis or ground for claiming to be entitled to either the salary or the residual payments or the reimbursements that he or she is claiming. So, given that the plaintiffs in the Pauley/Clark lawsuit worked on *Comics.TV* at different times and in different roles, we are actually dealing with a number of different issues rather than with a similar or common cause of a similar or common injury.

Long story short, all these factors will seriously increase the difficulty of managing the case as a class action. In the way class actions normally work, the plaintiffs in this case would have an easier time if they were hired at the same time or had performed the same kind of work, and yet ended up not getting paid. This is because the whole point of having class actions is to make it easier for folks in the same boat to pursue the same kind of relief or remedy. Class actions also help the courts to save both time and taxpayers' money by avoiding having to deal with the same kinds of claims over and over again when they could be done in just one shot.

So, it turns out that the plaintiffs, Pauley and Clark, won't have the easiest time mounting this case as a class action after all. But win or lose on the class action front, the plaintiffs are still very much in the game since they can always re-file their cases separately as individual claimants. Plus, their breach of contract claim is an entirely separate issue from the class action itself. Fortunately for the plaintiffs, they have a written agreement with their former employers, as they claim. Still, as with all written contracts, it is the terms of the contract that make all the difference in the end.

Concerning the claims in the present lawsuit, it will be most helpful to the comedian-plaintiffs if their contract is written not only in clear language but also in as much detail as possible. For instance, exactly what does the agreement say about salaries, residuals, and reimbursement of work-related expenses? The more clearly the contract is written, the less they'll have to deal with the hassle of lawyers bending and spinning the words used in the agreement to benefit their partisan points of view. Such a situation is never a good thing for somebody who is owed money, or who is trying to enforce some right or benefit given to him or her under a contract. So, the clearer the agreement is on these disputed matters, the better will be the chance that the court will agree with the plaintiffs that the monies are indeed owed to them.

Then again, it may be that the agreement is more complicated than that, especially with matters like the right of the plaintiffs to collect residual payments or reimbursement for work-related expenses. For instance, if as sometimes happens, the agreement contains a couple of things that must be done first before payment can be made (such things are called "conditions precedent"), then the person being sued could counterpunch from another front by claiming that the conditions precedent have not yet been fulfilled.

Speaking of work-related expenses, the comedians are claiming reimbursement for things like air-travel, car rentals, wardrobe, and gasoline expenses. Usually, these kinds of expenses are required to be reimbursed so long as they are not already included in the employees' regular compensation. Also, in situations where the staffers use their own phones or cars on their job or lay out their own monies for training or educational materials, they are usually reimbursed for them. But contracts aside, the laws of most states protect the employees' right to reimbursement of these expenses anyway. In California, where Allen does business, the labor code protects this right even more strongly than in many other states: in that state, once the employee is entitled to reimbursement, it is difficult to see how an employer can avoid paying it, even if the employee makes his claim rather late or miscalculates the amount of the claim. For that matter, even where he has already agreed to waive the claim, he can still turn around and collect it.

However, getting reimbursement money in these situations is not automatic. For instance, as already noted, if the expenses are already included in the staffers' compensation, then it cannot be claimed separately. Also, it may be important to see how Allen's side classified folks like Pauley and Clark in the course of their operations. If folks like the plaintiffs were considered as 'independent contractors' rather than as employees, then they would not have the right to reimbursement of work-related expenses. Unlike an employee, an independent contractor does his job as required under the contract but is not subject to the control and supervision of the person who hires him when it comes to the way and manner in which he performs the work. So, because an independent contractor works for himself and decides on his expenses all by himself, the question of the reimbursement of his work expenses usually does not arise.

With respect to the reimbursement claim in this case, if there is a dispute as to whether Pauley and Clark were regarded as independent contractors during their work for *Comics.TV*, the question can be answered by simply looking at the terms of their written agreement. And if it is not clear from the agreement itself, then one can look at the way the parties either worked with each other or treated each other during the time the plaintiffs worked on the show to see if they acted as though they were independent contractors.

There is one more thing in this case: Pauley and Clark reportedly claim that they were told by their union and their agents that they would be receiving residual payments from Allen's side. If the agreement they signed with Allen's company does not provide for residual payments, then it won't help that their handlers and associates promised them they would receive such monies. That just won't cut it, unless it emerges that their union or their agents had signed a separate agreement with Allen's side in which the plaintiffs were given the status of "third-party beneficiaries" with respect to residual payments.

A third-party beneficiary is an outsider to a contract who is given a benefit by the parties making the contract. Because such an outsider has been given some right or interest under the contract, he can actually file a lawsuit to claim the benefit he has been given under the contract, even though he was not one of the parties who had made the contract. The typical example here is the beneficiary of a life insurance policy. In our case here, Pauley and Clark can sue for residual payments if they can somehow qualify as third-party beneficiaries, assuming, of course, that there is a contract between their union and agents and Allen's side.

In the end, this case will go forward either as a class action or as a regular breach of contract action being pursued by separate plaintiffs. Yet because it has been filed as a class action, the outcome of this case will be watched by folks other than just the parties involved. At the minimum, one can imagine that the producers of the many successful comedy and entertainment shows on TV who enjoy big production budgets will be interested to see how things shake out here. What usually happens in real life is that when going up against such big money TV shows, aggrieved staffers would much rather do such heavy lifting in the form of a class action than as individuals. One big reason here is that class action folks are often in a great position to attract lawyers who are willing to represent them on a contingency basis, especially if the money numbers make sense to lawyers.

In any event, regardless of how things move forward here, given that there is a written agreement between the parties, if the case doesn't settle before the trial, the question of who wins or loses will depend on what the actual terms of the contract are. As always, in situations like this, the devil is in the details.

THE RIGHT OF COMEDIANS TO FREE SPEECH

CHAPTER TWO

THE RIGHT OF COMEDIANS TO FREE SPEECH

This chapter covers situations where a comedian got in trouble for things they said onstage and sometimes for things they said offstage while acting or speaking in the role of a comedian. Whether it is Jim Norton driving some lawyer nuts by joking about him wanting to have sex with a chicken, or Jay Leno alienating the Sikhs with his Mitt Romney joke or Joel McHale messing with the married dwarfs Cara and Gibson Reynolds, there is little doubt that comedy can and does get pretty offensive sometimes, especially from the point of view of people who may feel humiliated or ridiculed by what was obviously said in comic jest. (Recall the infamous slap heard around the world involving actor Will Smith and comedian Chris Rock during the 94th Academy Awards ceremony in Los Angeles on March 27, 2022.)

Yet, from all indications, if there is one thing that the cases in this section make crystal clear, it is quite simply that America is the best place on earth that anybody can comfortably be in the business of funny without losing their shirt. Welcome to the world of the First Amendment and defamation. Let's take a look at some of the cases.

* * *

JERRY SEINFELD: A Comedian's Lesson
from a Defamation Case

New York
November 11, 2012

A few years ago, star comedian Jerry Seinfeld's family spent quite a bit of time in court and with lawyers. First, his wife gets sued for plagiarizing (or copying) somebody else's cookbook. Then Seinfeld himself gets sued for talking about the lawsuit filed against his wife when he appeared on David Letterman's show. And it is the same person that is suing them the whole time. In the end, though, the Seinfeld's got the last laugh: the wife beat back the lawsuit against her and then another court sided with Seinfeld in denying that he committed defamation against Missy Chase Lapine, the woman who had sued them.

Here's what happened: Around 2007, Lapine sued Jessica Seinfeld (Jerry's wife), for plagiarism, claiming that Seinfeld's cookbook *Deceptively Delicious*, which dealt with sneaking pureed vegetables into kids' food was copied from her own cookbook *The Sneaky Chef*. The case was dismissed because the court said that the two books were different enough from each other and that sneaking pureed stuff into kids' food wasn't such a big new idea after all. (The back story here is that publisher HarperCollins rejected Lapine's book twice before picking up Seinfeld's own book and helping her promote it on Oprah's show. The book turned into a hit.) Later that same year, Seinfeld himself appeared on *The Late Show with David Letterman* and without mentioning Lapine by name, said some unflattering things about her, including using such words as *wacko*, *stalker*, and *nut job*. At one point, Seinfeld said, "We're sorry that she's angry and hysterical and because she's a three-name woman. She has three names. And if you read history, many of the three-named people do become assassins. Mark David Chapman. And you know, James Earl Ray. That's what concerns me." Lapine then sued him for defamation, claiming that Seinfeld's use of the words: *wacko*, *stalker*, *nut job*, and *assassin* amounted to defamation.

Well, the court didn't agree with her, and Seinfeld's folks celebrated their good day in court. "Today's decision is a complete victory for Jerry, and also a victory for the First Amendment and the right of comedians to tell jokes," Orin Snyder, Seinfeld's lawyer said. Seinfeld's lawyer's gloating aside, the defamation portion of this case is the one that offers up a few good lessons to comedians on just how much space the law allows them to swing their arms when talking about other folks.

For starters, "context" is a big deal in a defamation case, especially because a typical defamation case tries to make the point that somebody else's false statement of fact had damaged the reputation of the person that is bringing the lawsuit. Since we are dealing with a statement of fact, it means that what the other person (the offender) said must be the kind of statement that can be shown to be true or false. If the statement is false, then the person making the statement is liable for defamation. But then again, a statement about somebody can either be a statement of fact or a statement of opinion. If the statement can be seen as a statement of opinion, then there is no defamation. And this is where the "context" (or in layman's language, the "circumstances") makes all the difference.

Whenever the law looks at the "context" of the statement, it does not do so through the eyes (or point of view) of the person suing or even the person being sued. Rather it looks at the statement through the eyes of what is known as a "reasonable person" in the community, and this is usually someone who would be unbiased, owing to the fact that he is not involved with any of the parties in the case.

When a comedian is being sued for something that he said, the whole talk of "context" and the difference between "fact" and "opinion" becomes an even bigger deal. As one might expect, comedians, more than any other group of folks out there, would be likely to benefit from this kind of analysis. The simple reason is that comedians are jokesters trying to draw a laugh and most people understand them to be just trying to draw a laugh. And in Seinfeld's case he obviously got the full benefit of being a comedian, and a well-known one at that. Here, everything was in a good place for Seinfeld: he was a comedian by profession; he was appearing on an entertainment show dominated by comedy and hosted by a well-known comedian, and he was speaking before a late-night audience looking to be entertained, including those watching at home.

Now, how is a reasonable person supposed to look at statements made in such a "circumstance"? Well, the court applied the "context" test, and flat out said that no reasonable viewer "would have believed that Seinfeld's statements were conveying facts about Lapine." The court added that no viewer could have regarded Seinfeld's statement as an accusation that Lapine was a would-be assassin or was in any way dangerous. In short, the court concluded that Seinfeld's statement on the *Late Show* were simply statements of opinion and not of fact.

That was the end of the road for Lapine's defamation claim, and it offered yet another proof of how hard it is to make a defamation case stick against a comedian thanks to the First Amendment and the right of free speech. But does it mean that somebody can't win a defamation claim against a comedian? The simple answer is that, as hard as it may be and despite their advantages in defamation court, comedians can still be found liable for defamation, because just like other citizens, they might sometimes slip up on a banana peel of legal liability.

To be sure, the First Amendment does not give anyone the license to break the law. When it comes to defamation, the general rule is that a person is not allowed to "murder another person's reputation in jest." And here, comedians stand in the same shoes as everyone else.

Again, "context" or "circumstances" play a big role on the flip side. We're talking about the same "context" factor that often allows comedians to beat most defamation raps. Thus, when the context or circumstances of the statement make it look like the comedian is stating a "fact" about somebody else, then the comedian will be liable for defamation if that statement of fact happens not only to be "false" but also damages the other person's reputation in the community. In such a case, just because the comedian accompanied the statement with a joke will not save him from being liable in defamation. So, the line will be crossed when the humor or joke is simply being used to mask or hide an attempt to injure somebody else's reputation. To be clear, we are talking only about statements of facts here. And by the way, if the statement of fact happens to be true, then the comedian or whoever made the statement will be protected from liability, just like in any other defamation case. Of course, as already noted above, when the statement is a matter of opinion, then the comedian will not be liable.

In Seinfeld's case, looking at everything from the eyes of a reasonable person, the court simply didn't buy the narrative that the comedian was making a statement of fact about Lapine or that he was expressing anything other than his own personal opinion about Lapine. None of those situations are enough to make him liable for defamation. Yet just because a person was appearing on a comedy or entertainment talk show doesn't necessarily mean that they won't ever be found liable for defamation. They can still get in trouble for defamation if they state something as a "fact" despite knowing that it was a false statement.

In the end, it's worth repeating that the real lesson from the Seinfeld case is that comedians are indeed allowed a lot of room for maneuver when it comes to defamation. And thanks to the First Amendment, that room is much larger in America than every place else. Yet, while they have room to say an awful lot about other folks, they don't have the kind of room that allows them to say just about anything. "A lot of room" and "unlimited room" are two different things. In perspective, because Seinfeld as a celebrity comedian has the kind of media connections and pretty big microphone that Lapine did not have, maybe it was bad manners and a case of unfair play on his part to have knocked his adversary on the *Late Show*, a national forum in which she had no opportunity to hit back at him. Perhaps some might even think that he acted a little like a schoolyard bully. Yet, fair or not, Seinfeld was still operating within the large room space available to comedians in the American public square. Long story short, what he did doesn't amount to defamation in law.

JIMMY KIMMEL: Teaching the "Rabbi" a Lesson

New York
January 10, 2012

Jimmy Kimmel is a star of late-night TV, and his star is still rising. Next up, he'll be hosting the White House Correspondent's Dinner in April. So, no one can doubt Kimmel's high profile in pop culture. But as a comedian he also gets into cheeky territory with stuff that really gives people the needle. And of course, in situations like that, trouble is never too far from the door. All sorts of trouble, that is. But Kimmel is not the sort of guy who's afraid of trouble and he pushes back hard when it comes his way. Just like he did recently this past December when he got the court to toss a lawsuit brought against him by somebody that he made fun of on his show.

Here's what happened: In the summer of 2010 basketball star LeBron James visited an orthodox Jewish rabbi named Yishayahu Yosef Pinto for spiritual guidance as he struggled to make a big decision on commercial endorsement deals. On an episode of his show in August 2010, Kimmel made a joke about the James-Pinto visit by showing a video clip of the event alongside a YouTube video of a rabbi named David Sondik, known on YouTube as the "Flying Rabbi." The Sondik video was meshed with a video of Kimmel himself sitting in a car and talking to Sondik (the Flying Rabbi) who was standing at the window of Kimmel's car and supposedly counseling Kimmel in incomprehensible sounds and wild manic gestures. Kimmel set up the joke as a way to communicate to his viewers that what LeBron James (who didn't speak any Hebrew) did on his visit to Rabbi Pinto (who himself didn't speak any English) made no more sense than what Kimmel himself had done with the Flying Rabbi.

For his part, Rabbi Sondik didn't find the joke funny, so he sued both Kimmel and ABC seeking damages for defamation, invasion of right of publicity, misappropriation of likeness and for copyright infringement. Sondik claimed that by portraying his voice, picture, and likeness as that of Rabbi Pinto he was made to "look foolish" and was cast as a "laughingstock."

A win for Sondik could have a pretty major impact on how far comedians on late night TV could go in running any video clips as part of a joke on people and events in the society. This could present a classic "slippery slope" situation for comedians: it would mean that every time comedians employ that technique on their show—that is, meshing different images or splicing stuff together—as part of their monologue, they have to worry about whether they have crossed the line into the lawsuit zone where folks like Sondik might be waiting for them. Incidentally, this practice has become so well established as an aspect of late-night TV satire that audiences have come to take it for granted on the Leno, Letterman, Conan, and other shows.

But Sondik obviously ended up losing, and so late-night TV satire as we know it will go on. The reason Sondik lost his case is pretty much the same reason that most people would not even launch a lawsuit like that to begin with. The court in this case made it crystal clear to him. The court basically said that the segment that Sondik was griping about was really just an attempt by Kimmel to make a satire of Lebron James' meeting with Rabbi Pinto, an event that by itself was either 'newsworthy or a matter of public interest'. Since Sondik's lawsuit was also sort of heavy on the right of publicity and misappropriation of likeness stuff, the court shot down that angle by stating that the Kimmel video clip had not been meant for "commercial use." The logic here is that newsworthy stuff and commercial stuff don't usually run in the same stream.

Long story short, Kimmel ended up making this one a cakewalk. What this confirms yet again is just how very difficult it is to win against a comedian for something done in the way of a joke. For starters, pretty much everyone understands that a comedian is just making a joke and therefore is not dealing with matters of fact in the real world. In this very case, any average late night TV viewer who saw that particular video clip would likely not have thought that Kimmel in fact met with the Flying Rabbi the way that Lebron James met with Rabbi Pinto. In short, comedians do splice stuff together in a funny way just to make people laugh and folks do get the joke on that. Simple as that!

Considering the media buzz and speculations about LeBron James' next career move in the NBA at the time of the meeting with Pinto, his decision to meet with Pinto was obviously both newsworthy and a matter of public interest. And such events are fair game for comedic gags. The way the court saw it, the meeting between James and Pinto was the main focus of the video clip by Kimmel rather than the Sondik bit in the clip. In this way of looking at it, it is obvious that not even LeBron James himself or Rabbi Pinto, for that matter, could have won a lawsuit against Kimmel for the video clip that Sondik sued about.

Speaking of matters of public interest, one might perhaps wonder whether it is fair that Sondik, who claims to be a private guy, should be dragged into a joke being made by Kimmel about public figures. To be sure, most folks would agree that LeBron James being a public figure should bear the consequences of any newsworthy events that his actions could generate. For that matter, so should Rabbi Pinto for getting involved with a public figure like James in a newsworthy event. But can it not fairly be said that Sondik was simply dragged into the whole thing and, as he claims in his lawsuit, made a "laughingstock" of?

Maybe so. But in America, parody is so heavily protected by the First Amendment that sometimes even innocent bystanders (and private persons) are swept along by its broad brush. In those situations when it all gets a bit messy, alas, there is no First Amendment protection for anyone against being made into a "laughingstock" or being made to "look foolish." Yet, the First Amendment has its place, and most Americans probably feel grateful that it exists, despite its occasional rough edges.

But here's the final picture: thanks to the protection of parody under the First Amendment, yet another comedian has won a shoving match against folks who don't like his sense of humor. And surely, the beat goes on for Jimmy Kimmel.

SUING JOHN OLIVER FOR DEFAMATION:
A Good Use of Time?

West Virginia
August 6, 2017

Speaking of occupational hazards, comedians cannot help but irritate people, and they do it aplenty. For what it is worth, they do get sued by those they piss off. This time John Oliver, host of HBO's *Last Week Tonight*, has been sued for defamation by Robert Murray, founder and CEO of coal company Murray Energy Corporation, over statements that Oliver made on his show in mid-June.

So, there we go yet again, along the beaten path, one might say, as another lawsuit is filed against a comedian over what he said on a comedy show. While it may be tempting for those with money and other resources to step out there and try to teach a comedian a lesson, one must wonder whether such a move is a good use of time in a place like America. But first, here's what happened:

On the aforementioned episode of his show, Oliver had a segment in which he knocked the Trump Administration's efforts to revive the coal industry and portrayed CEO Murray as a guy who had fought against coal safety regulations. He referenced the collapse of one of Murray's mines in Utah in 2007, in which nine miners were killed, plus how Murray falsely claimed that an earthquake was to blame for the disaster even though, as Oliver said, a government report indicated otherwise.

In response, a few days later, Murray sued John Oliver along with the show's producer Charles Wilson, HBO, and parent company Time Warner on the claim that the segment was "false, injurious and defamatory" and that it was based on the show's biases against the coal industry and the Trump Administration's coal policies. To support his suit, filed in [coal country] West Virginia, Murray, whose company is based in Ohio, claimed that the show's producers were fully aware that a report by a government agency (Federal Mine Safety and Health Administration) supported his own version of the events and yet persisted in running the segment that "intentionally, falsely, and outrageously" asserted that Murray's claim was false.

So, that's Murray's defamation case against Oliver. But what are his genuine chances of winning? Well, for starters, defamation involves a false statement of fact that results in injury to somebody's reputation or standing in the community. Now, in defending this case, Oliver appears to have two grounds upon which he can push back against Murray. In other words, he can actually get two bites at the apple.

First, since we are dealing with an alleged false statement of fact, it follows that "truth" is a recognized defense to any defamation claim. And, given the circumstances of this case, one can predict that Oliver will try to play the truth card. Prior to the show episode in question, Murray's side had served a "cease-and-desist" notice on Oliver's people demanding that they not run the offending segment. Yet, during the show, Oliver positively scoffed at Murray's notice, saying, "I know that you're probably going to sue me, but you know what? I stand by everything I said." So there you have it: Oliver clearly anticipated this lawsuit as well as his likely use of truth as a shield against liability. Translation: "The truth shall set you free...", as the saying goes.

Then again, what if for some reason the truth defense doesn't fly? Does it mean Oliver is toast? Not so fast! Now since we're living in America, he could then move the ball into First Amendment territory, where our nation's high court has long since held that debate on matters of public policy must be "uninhibited, robust, and wide open." Under the law here, for Murray to win, he has to show that Oliver knowingly made a false statement of fact or that he was reckless as to whether or not the statement was true. This is the so-called "actual malice" standard, which applies to public figures.

Now, Murray may not be a public official, but it is hard for him not to be classified as a "public figure" considering a number of factors ranging from his prominent role in the mine collapse controversy and the references to him during official hearings on the matter, to his position as the CEO of what is regarded by many as the biggest privately owned coal company in America. (He would at least qualify as a "limited public figure," and that's good enough for this purpose.) Besides, this is a debate about an important matter of public policy and concern, namely, mine safety. So, yeah, in this lawsuit Murray probably will be deemed a public figure subject to the actual malice test. Therein lies a big problem for him because this test typically is a high hurdle for anyone to clear and, as experience has shown, the analysis here is exactly where these sorts of cases usually meet their Waterloo.

This is also notwithstanding Murray's allegation that the show's producers in pushing their biased version of events were aware of other reports which indicated that an earthquake was responsible for the mine collapse. If Oliver relied on a government report in forming his opinion on the matter, as he claimed, then he cannot be said to have acted with malice, a la reckless disregard of the truth. As a participant in a public policy debate, he was entitled to hold and advance his own opinion, however offensive it may be.

Yet, if all else fails (which is unlikely anyway), Oliver can always say he was just making a joke as (you guessed it!) a comedian. Here, as long as a comedian is understood by his listeners to be making a joke, it makes it that much harder for a defendant like Murray to claim that the listeners are taking the funnyman's cracks as true statements of fact, especially when we're dealing with a famous comedian.

Oh, by the way, speaking of making a joke as a comedian, Oliver could also simply decide to play his entire defense backwards from the way it has been presented above. So, he could, for instance, straight up claim that the whole thing was all a joke for the amusement of his listeners. And if that doesn't cut it, he can then start taking his two bites at the apple as described above, namely, that the offending statements are "true" anyhow or, alternatively, that he was just participating in an "uninhibited, robust, and wide-open" debate on a matter of public concern.

In the end, there are a couple different ways that Oliver could win this thing. On the flip side, Murray's odds of winning are quite long indeed. Then again, Murray could be the sort of guy who finds it worth his while to hale Oliver into court and make him sweat some and spend money on lawyers. After all, the statements in his lawsuit suggest that Murray feels wounded by Oliver's attempts to make fun of his age and appearance. Recall that Oliver also called the guy a "geriatric Dr. Evil," for added measure. So, given the gigantic odds against him, it is quite possible that Murray might choose to press ahead in this lawsuit because he looks at victory in an altogether different way, however perverse and vindictive that might seem to the rest of us. Otherwise, a lawsuit of this sort against a comedian in a place like America isn't a good use of time, because winning on the merits just isn't a realistic expectation.

CASE UPDATE: In late February 2018, the court in West Virginia dismissed Robert Murray's defamation lawsuit against John Oliver on the grounds that Oliver's actions were protected by the First Amendment. Despite his victory, Oliver didn't exactly break out the champagne in celebration: the lawsuit reportedly cost him more than $200,000 in legal fees and caused his show's libel insurance premiums to go up threefold. Being a deep pocket, perhaps, punishing Oliver in this way was Murray's goal the whole time.

JIM NORTON: Lessons from a "Chicken" Defamation Fight

New York
October 10, 2011

Comedian Jim Norton and the *Opie and Anthony Show* are two of a kind. When they come together, it may be wise to prepare oneself for a moment that may not be so ordinary. As it happens, Jim Norton is a stand-up comic who is known for pushing a tough line with foul-mouth remarks that draw blood; for its part, the *Opie and Anthony* radio show itself is a no-holds-barred arena. Their collaboration is something of a perfect storm for words that may hurt, sting, and irritate—and for a potential defamation lawsuit to boot. And that's exactly what came to pass when Roy Den Hollander, a self-styled "anti-feminist lawyer" sued Norton for defamation.

To be sure, Hollander is a gadfly Manhattan lawyer who is no stranger to controversy. He claimed he had called into the show in the hope of having an intelligent discussion of the merits of his lawsuit against Columbia University in which he was seeking to have the university abandon its women's studies program. Earlier on, he had filed but lost a lawsuit in which he sought to have the nightclubs cancel their "Ladies Night" sessions.

But here's what happened: During Hollander's call-in participation on an episode of the *Opie and Anthony Show*, hosted by Norton in 2009, an argument had broken out between the two. In the heat of their testy exchange, Norton berated Hollander as a "stupid" person and a "whore" who desired to have sex with a feathered fowl. According to Hollander, the most offensive remark made by Norton was the part where Norton said: "The chicken crossed the road because it thought that [Hollander] would try to f*ck it."

Not wanting to let things slide, Hollander filed a defamation lawsuit against Norton, seeking a half-million dollars in damages.

In his suit, Hollander claimed that Norton's crude remarks "held him up to public contempt and disgrace and caused him personal humiliation, mental anguish, and suffering."

For his part, Norton filed a motion asking the court to sanction Hollander for filing a baseless lawsuit and also for Hollander to pay Norton's legal fees.

Sensing disaster ahead, Hollander decided to cut his losses and soon the parties settled the case, with each side agreeing to drop its demands against the other. Despite the settlement, Hollander insisted he would have won the case anyway, even though he said he believed the judge in the case was unsympathetic to his claim: "The judge wasn't too favorable towards the case, so I decided to quit while I was ahead…I figured Norton's learned his lesson and he won't mouth off as much…you don't always have to win a case to win a case."

At any rate, the case settled. But could Hollander have won his defamation lawsuit against Norton? Not likely, and it was smart of him to quit when he did.

For starters, considering that their line of work requires comedians to make fun of other people and of the society itself, most people won't be too surprised to find that a defamation lawsuit would be the most common occupational hazard for comedians. When any person sues somebody else for defamation, he pretty much would be claiming that his reputation in society has been injured or damaged by something the other person said about him. But to win his case, the person suing has to show that the person being sued made a "false statement of fact." This means he cannot win his case if the statement is a statement of "opinion" rather than "fact." Of course, if the statement happens to be "true," then he cannot win, no matter how much damage the statement does to his reputation.

And since we are talking about damage to reputation in society, what matters in a defamation claim is what the society itself thinks: Would most reasonable people in society who hear the statement think of it as an expression of fact or just an opinion? As it happens, most people tend to view comedians as folks who make a parody of other people as well as the society itself just to draw a laugh. They certainly don't see them as people who are expressing facts. And it's mostly for this reason that suing a comedian for defamation is a pretty difficult business.

It's the rare occasion where a defamation lawsuit against a comedian succeeds—as happened this past July in Australia where the Channel Ten television station in Australia was fined for allowing comedian Mick Molloy to joke on the station's football TV show *Before the Game* that a female politician named Nicole Cornes, who was married to a former football coach, had slept with a former football player. The Australian court accepted the claim that the broadcast was an attack on a woman's "self-respect and dignity" and rejected the excuse that given the humorous context of the show, the joke was not meant to be taken literally. But that was Australia. In America, it would have been a more difficult case for Cornes because of the First Amendment's free speech provisions. Given that she is a politician, she probably would have been regarded as a "public official/public figure," and a tougher test called "actual malice" would have been applied to her case. (Still, she'd probably be more likely than not to win in the end.)

One big lesson from the Norton case is that suing a comedian in defamation, as tempting as it may be, is no easy business, even with comedians as outrageous as Norton. But while that may be a lesson for everyday folks out there, most people would expect that somebody like Hollander, a controversial lawyer, who's been around for a while with these kinds of stuff, would already know that lesson. It's safe to say that Hollander's defamation lawsuit against Norton is quite frivolous, and as it happens, not a few people could see that. The judge in the case clearly saw that, and Hollander himself knew the judge saw it as well. The lawsuit was a boneheaded idea, and Hollander could certainly have used his time better. Rather than teach Norton a lesson, as he claimed, it was Hollander himself, it seems, who had, quite surprisingly, forgotten an old lesson.

THE JAY LENO TRIANGLE: Comedy, Courtroom, and Foreign Relations

California
February 10, 2012

Funnyman Jay Leno is back in court, and we've seen this script before. Just last month, the Sikh religion found itself at the butt of Leno's jokes, and the Sikh faithful simply did not find the stuff amusing. So, early the next week, Randeep Dhillon, an Indian American and a Sikh, filed a defamation lawsuit in Los Angeles against both Leno and NBC for allegedly 'racist' remarks that defamed the Sikh religion and injured his feelings and those of other Sikhs. Dhillon claimed that Leno's remark exposed the Sikh religion to "hatred, contempt, ridicule, and obloquy because it falsely portrayed the holiest place in the Sikh religion as a vacation resort owned by a non-Sikh." Overseas, folks were not amused by the joke either: the Indian foreign ministry strongly condemned the joke as "quite unfortunate and quite objectionable" and vowed to take up the matter with the U.S. State Department.

It all happened during a monologue segment on Leno's *Tonight Show*, when the talk show host showed photos of the homes of Republican presidential candidates. When it came time to show multimillionaire Mitt Romney's pricey vacation home in New Hampshire, Leno instead showed a photo of the sprawling and majestic Golden Temple, in Amritsar, India, the most revered temple in the Sikh religion. Though Leno reaped boisterous laughter from his late- night audience he did hit a raw nerve and create ripples outside the world of comedy.

So, bingo! there we go again: another late-night guy, another monologue quip, another pissed off person, and another lawsuit.

In America, the lawsuit itself has not been well received and has, in fact, been ridiculed by many, including Fox cable TV's controversial host Bill O'Reilly who in his trademark derisive manner described the lawsuit as "dopey." One commentator, himself a lawyer, said the filing of the lawsuit was proof positive that there were indeed too many lawyers in America.

It turns out that the Americans and the Indians view both the joke and the lawsuit rather differently. But politics and cultural differences aside, does the lawsuit look like something that might have legs in the courtroom? Well, in America at least, it seems like Dhillon's chances of winning his lawsuit may be quite close to zero.

For starters, suing somebody for defamation in America is a whole different ball of wax from suing that same person anywhere else. Especially a public figure like Leno, and especially on a matter so connected to politics as the wealth of political candidates. Throw in the religion factor, and the whole thing gets messy pretty fast. Plus, the man is, of all things, a comedian, to boot. In these situations, the First Amendment comes across like an 800-pound gorilla sitting in the courtroom. At its heart, the First Amendment is all about promoting an atmosphere of "uninhibited, robust, and wide-open debate" about matters of public concern.

Considering that Leno is a comedian, the defamation lawsuit has two big strikes against it in a place like America. First, what Leno did in his monologue was an attempt to "parody" the economic background of candidates running for political office. For whatever it is worth, such a "satirical" treatment of current events usually gets a ton of protection from the First Amendment.

Also, Leno being a comedian, his remarks during his monologue were not understood as statements of fact but mere jokes by a comedian trying to get a laugh. Since in a defamation case the person filing the lawsuit is claiming that his reputation in the community has been damaged by the false statement made by the person he is suing, the "context" of the statement itself becomes quite important. And this is where it gets quite difficult for someone like Dhillon. Speaking of "context", the monologue segment of

The Tonight Show is clearly understood by most everyone in America as an occasion for lighthearted jokes designed merely to make people laugh and no more.

This means that even those audience members at Leno's show who had never seen or heard of the Sikh's Golden Temple would have simply taken it that Leno was just making a joke about Romney's wealth. Such an image, by itself and in association with Romney, would not have caused those audience members to hold the Sikh religion up for "hatred, contempt, ridicule, and obloquy." Plus, even setting aside the "context" of the statement for the moment, it is also fair to say that neither Dhillon himself nor any other person, (whether they are Sikhs or otherwise) who truly knows the Golden Temple, could have really thought that the place shown in the photo on Leno's show was, in fact, Romney's home.

Speaking of what claims Dhillon could make against Leno, perhaps in other circumstances, he might be able to sue for a tort called Intentional Infliction of Emotional Distress on the claim that the joke was "extremely outrageous" and thereby "intolerable in a civilized society." Yet, in a place like America where comedy is a huge part of the pop culture, Dhillon's big problem is that he'd have to demonstrate that the joke was both extremely outrageous and utterly intolerable in a society like America. Fat chance! And there's always the First Amendment, still sitting in the courtroom.

Of the two hurdles that are set against this case, the First Amendment issue is the bigger one. Incidentally, not even Romney himself could win this kind of lawsuit in an American court. The protection for "satire" under the First Amendment is so broad that even hurtful, unnecessary, and outrageous remarks are protected. It's interesting that the Indian foreign ministry, in condemning Leno's remarks, also added that "freedom does not mean hurting the sentiments of others." Well, maybe so, but in the American experience, it happens apparently.

None of this stuff is new to Americans. For example, thanks to the First Amendment, attacks on other people's religions by both comedians and other folks are not punished by the law. If there is any surprise in this whole situation, it perhaps ought to be that Dhillon, an American himself, could indeed have expected to win this kind of lawsuit. This being America, the Catholic Church, for instance, or perhaps the Mormon religion for that matter, would not have thought it worth their time to file a defamation lawsuit against Leno if the image he had used on his show for Romney's home would have been instead a Catholic cathedral or some iconic Mormon building.

Though such a depiction would obviously piss off those religious organizations and definitely rub them the wrong way, lawsuits in situations like that just don't work out here in America, regardless of whether or not they should. One remarkable example comes to mind here. Not long ago, in the wake of the child sex abuse scandals that rocked the Catholic Church, comedian Louis CK put out a You Tube clip in which he accused the entire Catholic Church of existing "solely for the purposes of boy rape." Well, nobody thought to sue him. Say hello to life in America under the First Amendment.

As already noted, the case has pretty long odds of success and will most likely fail when push finally comes to shove in the courtroom. But before the courts weigh in, the foreign policy people have already given their short answer to the question in this case. In typical America-speak, the State Department has let it be known in an official statement that what Leno did was protected by the First Amendment. (Of course, the State Department also acknowledged the tensions that the joke has caused to the friendly relations between the U.S. and India.) It is only a matter of time before the courts tell Dhillon the same thing about the First Amendment.

In the end, this one seems like a total no-brainer. The way it is, diplomacy and foreign relations have their place, but Leno is just a comedian trying to make people laugh on his show. And it is a safe bet that none of this entire hoopla will be slowing him down any time soon: If the stuff is funny, it seems like the funnyman will take his shot, diplomatic sensibilities and foreign relations be damned. That's just the way things can be with comedy and, as they often like to say, "It's nothing personal!"

JAY LENO: "Woulda, Coulda, Shoulda," He Pay for Defamation?

New York
November 27, 2013

Jay Leno knows a thing or two about the occupational hazards of a comedian's work. In the new book *Comedy Under Attack: The Golden Age and the Headwinds*, one comedy industry insider reportedly remarked that stand-up comedy is 'the most fun anyone can have with their clothes on.' Well, at least until somebody else gets offended. When those situations arise, a couple of things could happen to the offending comedian: perhaps a mobster in the comedian's audience would corner him in the hallway near the bathroom and threaten to break his legs unless he admits he's not funny (think Jimmy Brogan). Or maybe he'll simply get sued in court if he's lucky. Let's just say that Jay Leno has better luck than his comedy colleague Jimmy Brogan – Leno is getting sued instead—for defamation. Here's what happened.

First, a former American Airlines flight attendant named Louann Giambattista sues her former employers claiming that she was wrongly accused by her co-workers of smuggling her pet rats onto the plane using her underwear or panty hose. Then Leno picks up the story in a segment of *The Tonight Show,* which he calls "Woulda Coulda Shoulda." There, he sets up the story and invites three other comedians to say what's on their mind about it. What followed wasn't exactly flattering to the former flight attendant: there was a crack about her sitting the rat in her 'cooch'; then a remark by another comedian that the flight attendant enjoys the idea of having 'creepy things' in her underwear, followed by a suggestion that she 'hook up' with comedian Jim Norton who'd made the remark; plus, yet another remark suggesting that she ought to be using a "rabbit" like other women instead of a rat. ("Rabbit" is a brand of vibrators for masturbation.)

Taking offense at all this, Giambattista sued Leno himself, *The Tonight Show,* and NBC Universal for defamation, claiming that that the joke falsely accused her of "engaging in bestiality and sexual misconduct with a rat." She alleged that the jokes amounted to 'sickening, outrageous, and disgusting" attacks on her character and that Leno essentially enabled the defamation by indulging those comments and laughing at the jokes. Giambattista claimed that as a result of the millions of folks who saw the joke, she and her husband have not only become "pariahs" in their community, but that their sex life has also been damaged due to her husband experiencing severe "sexual dysfunction" from thinking back to the way Leno had portrayed her as a 'sexual deviant." (Not that she needed to, but curiously, she didn't choose to join as parties to her lawsuit any of the comedians who made the allegedly offensive remarks.)

So, do we have something serious here or is this just another weak defamation shot aimed at a comedian by someone who just can't take a joke? Well, not if she can win.

In a defamation action, the idea is that the defendant (the person being sued) has damaged the reputation of the plaintiff (the person suing) in the community by the use of false statements. Usually, as part of the protest against the defendant's attack on his or her reputation, the plaintiff tags on a claim for money damages. This is pretty much what the plaintiff here (Giambattista) is trying to do against Leno and the other defendants, as she claims damages against them plus her lawyers' bills and more.

But then, why is she suing Leno in New York rather than in Los Angeles where Leno lives and does his show? This is a question that some comedy fans have asked me, wondering if she can actually do that. The short answer is that yes, she can! As the law stands, one of the reasons why a plaintiff in a civil action, such as defamation, can sue a defendant at a particular location is that such location is where the wrongful action complained about took place. This means that if Leno's actions in California damaged Ms.

Giambattista's reputation in her neighborhood in New York, then she can sue him in New York. Besides, we're talking about a late-night show that is seen across the country as well as online. Now, how about we stretch the question a bit further since we live in the internet age: What if Giambattista lived in Australia and her neighborhood folks over there saw Leno's show online? Can she sue Leno in Australia for damaging her reputation? Well, again, the answer is yes, at least in theory. Of course, as a practical matter, it'd be so much easier to file the lawsuit in the particular country where the defendant lives.)

Anyhow, the case was filed in New York and will go forward in New York. For starters, because Leno is a comedian and she is suing him for defamation, one of her biggest obstacles would be to prove that Leno's statement was false in the way that the law of defamation demands. In this area, we're dealing only with statements of fact. We're also talking about the impact of the statement on those who heard it.

As everyone probably understands, a *fact* is something that can be proven to be either true or false. For example, whether a particular car is red or black is a matter of fact since we can tell that from simply looking at the car. Same deal with somebody's height: this is a matter of fact since it can simply be determined by measuring the person. However, statements like whether someone is a jerk, or a really great guy are not exactly things that can be shown to be true one way or the other. One man's jerk may be another's hero. These kinds of subjective assessments or statements are regarded as *opinions* rather than facts, which are objective in nature. In defamation court, facts are in, and opinions are out. Simple!

Aside from facts and opinions, the other big question in defamation court is whether the statement itself was meant to be taken seriously or whether it was just something being said in jest and so could only have been understood by its listeners in that way. The reason here is pretty simple: If those who heard the statement thought it was just a joke and didn't take it seriously at all, then the notion that the statement caused them to think less of the plaintiff and to treat her as a pariah just won't wash. Besides, if the defendant in any defamation case would have simply made the statement to the plaintiff alone, and nobody else heard it, there will be no grounds for a defamation action.

So, where does all the stuff above leave our case? It's fair to say that when we combine the idea of an opinion and a joke, they add up to a long and difficult day in court for someone like Giambattista who is trying to pin a defamation rap on a well-known comedian like Leno. Many of these kinds of attempts against comedians have failed in the past, and this one isn't exactly looking much different from the rest. To be sure, most folks in Ms. Giambattista's position would be pretty offended by the crude remarks lobbed at her during that segment of Leno's show. All the talk about "cooch," "creepy things" in her underwear, and use of "rabbits" are obviously not pretty things to be said about a respectable lady on national TV. But context is very crucial in a defamation case: Leno is a comedian, and as the logic goes, he apparently meant all that stuff as a joke ,and most reasonable folks who saw or heard about that segment of his show probably understood it as a joke as well. An offensive joke is still a joke.

Yet the fact remains that life is hardly so black-and-white in all defamation cases. Sometimes the way jokes and facts mix with each other can get pretty dicey, especially when what was said is the kind of stuff that can be shown to be true or false. There is an old rule in defamation cases that no one is allowed to "murder" somebody else's reputation in jest. In fact, in the case from Australia mentioned previously in the Jim Norton story, a comedian had said on a sports television show that a married woman had had an affair with a football player on her husband's team; only problem is, it wasn't true. When push came to shove in court, he attempted to say that the statement was meant as a joke. But that argument was rejected, and he was found liable. And he received no help from the fact that the show itself had a reputation for regularly fielding humorous remarks from guests. By the way, if the Australian comedian would have simply described the woman as a bitch or something like that, for instance, then as offensive as that statement might be, it would simply be considered as an opinion, meaning that she likely wouldn't have been able to nail him for defamation. But he crossed the line instead by making a false statement of fact.

Obviously, since Leno's actions in this case are vastly different from what happened with the overseas comedian above, the idea in the above example that comedians can sometimes get in trouble for defamation will probably come only as cold comfort to someone like Giambattista. Nothing that Leno or any of his guests said on his show about her even approaches a factual statement that can be proven to be true or false. To the plaintiff's disadvantage, this all puts Leno safely back in the protected area of jokes and opinions where comedians are literally untouchable in defamation cases.

In the end, the outcome of a case like this one is quite predictable. Many of these cases follow a familiar pattern in the way they fall by the wayside. Fair or not, comedians seem to benefit the most from the free speech protections in American courtrooms, whether they are attacking public figures or whether they are in more risky situations where they are attacking private persons. The plaintiff's case here seems to fall in the cookie-cutter category where there are no aggravating circumstances that could make a difference to the outcome in court. In such situations, it is probably not the best use of time for anyone to be suing a comedian for defamation. Of course, if the person (plaintiff) has other goals in mind than actually winning the case, then all bets are off.

It is interesting to note that Giambattista's husband's job in the food industry also figures in the mix: It's been said that "the allegations against his wife have called into question whether he should be preparing food after contact with rats." Well, it's difficult to see how Leno's liability for defamation, even if it exists, could be stretched as far as that. But that is where we are with the allegations in this case. Whatever the plaintiff's motivations in this case, it is obvious that suing a huge celebrity like Leno could yield great publicity for anyone interested in the limelight. And if such a person is willing to pay his or her lawyers for their time, (who knows?) the game may well be worth the candle.

BRITAIN'S FRANKIE BOYLE: The Meaning of Defamation Across the Atlantic

Britain
July 13, 2013

Between the way the world thinks of him and the way he doesn't want anyone to think of him, the whole stuff about reputation seems to loom pretty large in British comedian Frankie Boyle's world. From all indications, the brash, irreverent comic doesn't seem to sweat what anyone calls him as long as no one calls him a "racist." In Boyle's worldview, for anyone to call him that amounts to something of a declaration of war. And he could hit the hapless aggressor pretty hard in the wallet and set the aggressor back by many thousands of pounds or dollars. At least, in Britain! Just ask the *Daily Mirror*, one of Britain's major tabloids, which took a big hit last fall for apparently "messing with the wrong marine," as the Americans would say.

On July 19, 2011, the *Daily Mirror* published an article in which it speculated about Boyle's chances of returning to his comedy show on Britain's Channel 4 television station: "Racist comedian Frankie Boyle could soon be returning to TV despite upsetting thousands of viewers with his sick jokes," began the article, which also claimed that Boyle was "forced to quit" the BBC panel show *Mock the Week* owing to his brand of comedy. Feeling deeply wounded by the article, Boyle sued the paper for defamation in a London court; he claimed that the article was defamatory and that it brought him into "odium and contempt" ⊠ stock phrases in many a defamation lawsuit. (By the way, to commit "defamation" against a person simply means to say things about that person which tend to damage or otherwise lower that person's reputation in the community. If those offending words appear in written form, the harm that results therefrom is known as a "libel," as in Boyle's situation.) Boyle claimed in court that just because he plays characters who express racist views doesn't mean that he himself is a racist. "These are phrases that a racist would use," Boyle said. "There is no way they are an endorsement of racist terminology. It is the absolute opposite of that." In support of Boyle's position, his lawyer stated that it would be "political correctness gone mad" if Boyle were labeled racist for using racial language in his jokes.

For its part, the paper showed no remorse over the publication and instead stuck to its guns, claiming that Boyle was a "racist comedian" who exploited negative stereotypes of black people for "cheap laughs." In a further slap at Boyle (who writes a column for rival newspaper *The Sun*), the *Mirror* told the jury that if they should find that Boyle had, in fact, been defamed, they should merely award him the sum of 45p (forty-five pence), the price of a copy of the *Daily Mirror*. Ouch! In the end, Boyle got the last laugh, as the jury found that the paper had indeed defamed him. As a result, the court awarded Boyle a total sum of more than ￼54,000 (more than $80,000 USD) in damages plus court costs against the *Daily Mirror*.

However, considering the close ties between the pop cultures of the British and American, not a few folks, especially in the comedy and media worlds, have wondered if Boyle could have won his case so brilliantly if he had brought the defamation lawsuit in America instead. For starters, if Boyle were merely a regular guy who either just drives a cab or works at the post office, his case probably would have gone the same way on both sides of the Atlantic. For example, if Pete defames Joe who is a private person (an average Joe) and Pete can't prove that what he said of Joe was true, then the defense fails, and Pete becomes liable to Joe for defamation. But where the situation involves a public figure (a celebrity), then the matter is handled in a different way in each country. And this is where Boyle, who is undoubtedly a public figure, would have faced a totally different ball game if the lawsuit would have been brought in the U.S.

It used to be that defamation cases were handled the same way on both sides of the pond until the 1960s when America decided that public officials and public figures would have to jump more hoops and work much harder than previously before they can win any defamation lawsuit that they choose to bring against anyone, whether a private person or a media organization. This meant that it is no longer just enough that something said about a public official or public figure was not true; a greater amount of fault on the part of the person who made the statement was now required. In short, a public official or public figure who files a defamation suit could still lose the case even if the statement made against him is later shown to be false.

This new rule is called the "actual malice test," and two things are required in order for someone to fail the test and thereby become liable for defamation when sued by a public official or a public figure: first, the person must have intentionally made or published the false statement with the knowledge that the statement was false; or second, that the person chose to make or publish the false statement when the circumstances were clearly such that he should have known that the statement he was making or publishing was false. (In this second scenario, you might include situations like someone, for instance, deliberately looking away from, say, another person who is trying to show him that the statement was false; or situations where someone simply chooses to believe some crazy "Mickey Mouse" kind of talk, as in, say, allowing themselves to believe that "pigs can fly." Instances that come under this second scenario are often regarded as "willful blindness.")

At the time the new rule of actual malice was adopted, it was said that the First Amendment, which commits America to the principle of "uninhibited, robust and wide-open debate" on matters of public interest or public issues, needed the new approach in order to provide greater protection for free speech. In the 1964 case where this new rule was established, the *New York Times* had published an ad put forward by an interest group; the said ad detailed the alleged mistreatment of civil rights activists by the Alabama authorities. It turned out that some of the facts stated in the ad were inaccurate, for example, how many folks had been arrested; exactly where the police had been positioned on the campus; what particular song the protesters had been singing and more.

When the public official in charge of the police sued the *New York Times* for defamation, America's High Court said it didn't matter that these statements of fact were in fact false. The court stated that under the First Amendment, no defamation was in fact committed as long as both the *Times* and those who paid for the ad didn't knowingly or intentionally publish the false statements nor did they publish them under circumstances where they clearly should have known that the statements were false.

So, as it happens, Americans are willing to put up with some 'false' stuff in order to protect the right to free speech and to preserve their highly prized culture of spirited debate on public affairs.

But why, in Britain, did Boyle win his case against the *Daily Mirror*? Well, it's fair to say that the jury simply didn't buy the defense's story: they didn't think it was true that Boyle was a racist or that he was "forced to quit" the *Mock the Week* show because of his racist views. The defense's style itself could be described as something of a "kitchen sink" strategy that allowed the defense to hedge its bets by playing the sort of hand that both an English lawyer and an American lawyer might choose to play in defending a case like this one. Essentially, the defense claimed that the offending statement was either "true" or was an "honest comment on a matter of public interest." Interesting tactic: first, to show that the statement was true, the defense trotted out some of Boyle's quite offensive remarks on the Channel 4 comedy show *Tramadol Nights*, including the infamous Madeleine McCann cracks about a missing child, plus his Twitter quips about Paralympic athletes. Then the defense came up with the public interest commentary that many an American defamation lawyer would recognize. Pretty smart hedge!

In hindsight, Boyle's opponents did not seem to have done themselves any favors with the whole *Mock the Week* business. It seems like the overall atmosphere at the jury trial tilted against them when they fought for but lost that branch of their case. For example, a witness with firsthand knowledge of the situation showed up at the trial to testify that Boyle was not in fact canned from *Mock the Week*. Even worse for the defense, the witness stated that the show's producers had hoped that Boyle would make a return appearance on the show in the future. Apparently, the *Daily Mirror* might have looked better just sticking with the general claim of racism against Boyle and no more.

But seriously, how would Boyle have fared in an American court? Short answer: Not as well as he did in Britain! Not even close. For starters, America, unlike Britain, is First Amendment country. So, predictably, the "public figure" business would have been front and center of this sort of case in an American court and with that (you guessed it!) comes the tough "actual malice" standard as well. All of this would have created massive complications for Boyle and thereby jeopardized his odds of winning. Incidentally, in the British case, the *Daily Mirror* won a small victory when it got the court to reject Boyle's claim of malicious falsehood in the *Mock the Week* imbroglio. In an American court, a ruling that there is no malice would be a huge factor that could only weigh down a public figure's odds of winning a defamation lawsuit against a newspaper which is defending itself on grounds of public interest.

In the end, considering the potential impact of these big issues on everyday life in any society, the Boyle-*Daily Mirror* case is one of those situations that remind any observer that, celebrations of "special relationship" aside, Britain and America are still different places after all. As far as comedy goes, America, thanks to the First Amendment, offers the safest harbor possible not only for anyone wishing to do comedy, but also for anyone in the mood to mess with comedians. In our case here, it means that a dude like Boyle, who would say anything about anyone but cannot stand for certain things to be said about him, obviously is living on the right side of the Atlantic—outside America, that is. For the *Daily Mirror*, well, living outside America apparently means a little less protection in defamation court.

FIGHTING THE DAILY STORMER: When a Comedian Sues a Rogue

Ohio
October 15, 2017

When a comedian sues a non-comedian for damaging his reputation, one can expect the sort of unusual scenario where the usual suspects become the ones trying to restore sanity. So, as the hunter becomes the hunted, and people wonder just how well the shoe will fit on the other foot, the recent case of Muslim comedian, lawyer, and liberal political commentator Dean Obeidallah against the controversial right-wing neo-Nazi website *The Daily Stormer* offers us a window into the reality of that tricky situation. But first, here's what happened.

This past June, Obeidallah, a SiriusXM radio host wrote a piece in *The Daily Beast* in which he queried why President Donald Trump wouldn't use the phrase "white supremacist terrorism" to describe the activities of right-wing extremists. According to Obeidallah, the defendant website responded by fabricating tweets that appeared to have been written by Obeidallah himself and posting an article titled "Dean Obeidallah, Mastermind Behind Manchester Bombing, Calls on Trump to Declare Whites the Real Terrorists." This was then followed by a torrent of online abuses directed at Obeidallah, even including death threats. Incidentally, Obeidallah and *The Daily Stormer* appear to be old enemies. Two years earlier, Obeidallah had written another piece in *The Daily Beast* in which he urged the GOP to disavow the growing support that then-presidential candidate Trump was receiving from right-wing extremist groups including (you guessed it!) *The Daily Stormer*.

In his lawsuit against *The Daily Stormer* and its publishers, chief among them (its public face) Andrew Anglin, Obeidallah seeks damages against the website for libel and intentional infliction of emotional distress.

Now, before even talking about Obeidallah's chances of winning this defamation lawsuit, it is worth considering something else, namely, that given the sort of folks that he's dealing with here, it increasingly looks like worrying about winning the case may well be the lesser of his problems. In fact, his biggest headache at this point is finding the people he is suing. Andrew Anglin and *The Daily Stormer*, for all their caustic advocacy of hate and extreme right-wing rhetoric, are notoriously shy when it comes to showing up to defend their position in court. And, whenever push comes to shove, finding them to serve them with court papers can often seem like looking for a tiny needle in a huge haystack. "Good luck finding them," one might well say to anyone in Obeidallah's position looking to serve Anglin and his website with court papers.

This past April, for instance, the Alabama-based nonprofit legal advocacy group, the Southern Poverty Law Center (SPLC) tried to serve *The Daily Stormer* with court papers after suing them for intentional infliction of emotional distress and invasion of privacy for allegedly orchestrating "a troll storm" that literally sought to destroy the life of Tanya Gersh, a Jewish real estate agent in Montana. (Supposedly, the Stormer's actions were aimed at punishing Ms. Gersh for engaging with the mother of white supremacist leader Richard Spencer.)

Let's just say that the report card on the SPLC's attempt to serve Anglin with court papers in his native Ohio at one point read like any plaintiff's nightmare: Seven different addresses and 15 return visits yielding nothing, plus lots of undelivered certified and regular mail service. (At one point, there was even a report, albeit unsubstantiated, on CNN that said Anglin had moved to Nigeria, of all places.)

Long story short, Obeidallah's opponents are not the easiest guys to find when it comes to serving court papers. Now let's get to the law on Obeidallah's claims against them.

First, the defamation claim involving injury to the plaintiff's reputation is fairly easy for anyone to understand. To call anyone a "terrorist" in our post- 9/11 world is a terrible thing. What's even worse is to say that of a Muslim person in a place like today's America. Under these circumstances, the damage to the plaintiff's reputation couldn't be more self-evident. For someone in the public eye like the comedian-plaintiff in this case, whose career survival and success depends to a large extent on his public image and his acceptance by the public, the label of "terrorist" is like a dagger to the heart of his reputation and standing in the society.

Of course, under the law, since truth is a defense to a defamation claim, a defendant can still defeat a defamation claim by showing that what he had said about the plaintiff is actually true. But, alas, such a defense is not available to *The Daily Stormer* in this case because what they said about Obeidallah is obviously an absolutely false and entirely made-up tale with the clear purpose of ruining his reputation.

Yet, since we're in America, the First Amendment could always come up as a defense in a defamation case. The neo-Nazi website, for instance, might attempt to claim that Obeidallah is a "public figure", and they were simply exercising some First Amendment free speech right on a matter of public concern. Speaking of public figures, Obeidallah may not be a familiar person to most people on the streets of America, but he's by no means merely the sort of anonymous [private] Joe out there who rides the subways of New York City on a routine basis. He's actually something of a controversial figure who takes on public causes. For instance, in the fall of 2015, he was one of the ringleaders of a group of comedians, including Negin Farsad, who won a lawsuit against the Metropolitan Transit Authority (MTA) allowing them to advertise their documentary *The Muslims Are Coming* in the New York City subways. In any event, public figure or not, any First Amendment defense attempted by *The Daily Stormer* in this case will all but flop on the simple ground that their statement against Obeidallah was "knowingly" false.

Now, how about the claim of intentional infliction of emotional distress, which, one might add, has grown into a staple of modern defamation cases? This claim is often designed to punish defendants whose actions are judged to be so "outrageous" as to "exceed all bounds of decency" and thus to be "utterly intolerable in a civilized society." Let's just say that for all the reasons stated above with respect to the defamation claim, the clearly outrageous actions of *The Daily Stormer* in this case should also make them liable for the intentional infliction of emotional distress.

In the end, for all the merits of his case, it's fair to say that Obeidallah is in something of a pickle, which is par for the course for anybody suing a rogue defendant like *The Daily Stormer* these days. He has overwhelming odds of winning the match if only he can get the other guy to show up. This is the kind of irony that one won't find in most regular cases where folks tend to worry less about their opponents actually showing up for the fight. Not to make light of the grave situation here, perhaps many of Obeidallah's comedy brethren might find in this ironic situation some good comedy material for their time onstage. But seriously, it'll be quite interesting to see how this case ends.

CASE UPDATE: As expected, Dean Obeidallah easily won the case. On June 12, 2019, the federal court awarded him the sum of $4.1 million as damages on his defamation claim against Andrew Anglin and his side. As one might have imagined, it was a "default judgment," meaning that the other side did not show up to participate in the proceeding. Needless to say, collecting on the said judgment is another whole ball of wax.

SACHA BARON COHEN BLINKS: How Not to Make a Comedy Movie

Washington, DC
August 11, 2012

Sacha Baron Cohen is a gifted comedy actor whose wacky sense of humor and the way he pushes the envelope in his movies often cracks up the audience big time. However, his shenanigans can sometimes seriously rub people the wrong way, even some of the folks in his hit movies. When that happens, the whole thing tends to come back to bite him in the neck, bringing with it some pretty bad PR, and perhaps even costing him some money. His latest headache just arrived from the Middle East, and this time even complete outsiders like talk show host David Letterman got themselves drawn into the mud fight. Here's what happened.

In 2010, a Palestinian grocer named Ayman Abu Aita who appeared in Cohen's 2009 hit comedy *Bruno* sued Cohen and the producers of the movie for over $100 million, claiming that the movie falsely portrayed him as a member of the Palestinian terrorist group Al-Aqsa Martyrs' Brigade. For his part, David Letterman, who was also named in Aita's defamation lawsuit against Cohen, was swept into the mess when Cohen appeared as a guest on Letterman's CBS late night show and talked about his interview with a Palestinian terrorist. In Aita's defamation suit, filed in Washington, DC, he claimed that the false portrayal of him in the movie had damaged both his reputation and his business and had brought on death threats against him and his family.

Aita claimed that when he gave an interview to Cohen during the shooting of the movie, he had thought he was speaking to an actual journalist about peace activism and didn't even realize he was taking part in a Hollywood movie. Aita claimed that he did not sign a "release" authorizing Cohen to include his image in the movie. (In the movie, Cohen, a Cambridge-educated-Brit, played an Austrian journalist on a mission to promote peace in the Middle East.).

As it happens, Cohen is no stranger to this kind of lawsuit and had actually been down this path before. In late 2006, in the aftermath of his blockbuster comedy *Borat*, the filmmakers were sued by two fraternity guys from the University of South Carolina who alleged that they were duped into appearing in the movie in which they made racist and sexist comments which they would never have made otherwise. The frat boys, who appeared in the movie as the traveling companions of Cohen's *Borat* character, claimed that the filmmakers had falsely told them that the movie would only be shown outside the United States.

But anyway, in the latest lawsuit filed against Cohen by somebody from his movies, an out-of-court settlement was reached this past July when Cohen figured he'd cut his losses rather than confront these serious allegations in a courtroom. The case was reportedly "settled to the mutual satisfaction of all the parties," though they would not disclose the terms of the deal. Despite the settlement, some have wondered what the final outcome might have been if Cohen had chosen to stay and fight. Could Cohen have had any good legs to stand on in court? Not quite, considering the law of defamation in America.

To begin with, Cohen and Letterman's folks made the smart choice to turn the whole thing into a free speech fight, which obviously offered them their best shot at defending the case. Their lawyers claimed that Aita's "name or likeness was used in a newsworthy context in a documentary-style movie that conveys matters of legitimate public interest." It's worth noting that the protection given to speech is very wide when someone is sued for defamation. Yet, the right to speak freely concerning "matters of public interest" is not unlimited, and the law draws the line on what is called "actual malice." In layman's terms, this mostly means that the person talking about free speech must show that he did not "in fact" know that he was "lying" when he said what he claims to have a free speech right to say. This is because the law of free speech is not meant to give anyone a license to "lie" or to deliberately peddle false information that damages other people's reputation—and this is exactly what the law of defamation is all about preventing folks from doing.

And this is where Cohen would have some real trouble in making his defense. As it happens, when Aita appeared in the movie *Bruno*, the caption on that particular scene read "Terrorist Group Leader, Al-Aqsa Martyrs Brigade." In the context of the scene, the description of Aita as a terrorist was presented as a statement of fact, not as an opinion. If the statement would have been presented instead as just an opinion, it would have made a big difference in Cohen's favor, especially because the *Bruno* movie is a comedy and America's First Amendment law can be described as a comedian's best friend.

But what happened in the *Bruno* movie was different; it was presented as a statement of fact that the man (Aita) was a member of a terrorist group. From all indications, when the scene was added to the movie, Cohen and the producers obviously knew that it was not true, especially since they had no reliable or even any source of information that the man was in fact a terrorist. As a matter of fact, it turns out that Aita is actually a Christian who had nothing to do with the Islamic terrorist group that he was said to be a leader of. So, given how little proof the filmmakers had that Aita was indeed a terrorist, we very likely are dealing here with a false statement of fact that was knowingly put in the movie. This would qualify as an "actual malice" situation that would seriously damage Cohen's chances of beating this defamation case on free speech grounds. Even if Aita were somebody in the public eye (such as a prominent national politician or an international celebrity), Cohen's chances of winning this case on free speech grounds would still be pretty weak.

Aside from all the free speech talk, there is the claim by Aita that he did not sign a release which would have legally authorized

Cohen and his team to include the man in their movie. If that's true, then apparently his participation in the movie was obtained by deception. Cohen's movie is a Hollywood product that is designed to make profits for the filmmakers, and there's a big difference between giving an interview to a journalist for a story about peace in the Middle East on the one hand and doing exactly the same thing as an actor participating in a Hollywood for-profit movie on the other. Using someone's image or likeness for a profit-making venture without that person's permission would give such a person a right to sue for damages for misappropriation of their publicity rights.

In hindsight, it seems that Cohen's decision not to obtain a signed release from Aita was a calculated move after all. The simple reason here is that a release agreement would probably have required Cohen's team to tell Aita what role he was being used for in the movie. It is easy to guess that Aita likely would not have agreed to be portrayed in the movie as a Palestinian terrorist, even though this was so obviously how Cohen's team appeared to want to use him in the movie.

Given the odds against Cohen in the lawsuit, it was probably smart thinking on his part to quit the fight early. It wouldn't have been a good case for someone in Cohen's position, and one can't help but think of the whole case as a teachable moment in how not to make a comedy movie. It's always better to let everyone in a comedy movie in on the joke and have them on the same page. Otherwise, it can cost the filmmaker money and bring him bad PR. It might even put lives at risk in certain turbulent regions of the world, such as Aita's neighborhood, where folks can actually get killed just because of what they say, unlike here in America. Most folks would hope that comedy can do better than that.

JOEL McHALE: A Sweaty Court Battle
with the Angry Dwarfs

Pennsylvania
November 10, 2011

Funnyman Joel McHale is a TV show host who pulls no punches when he takes the bat to celebrities and reality TV stars. But some of his targets are not the kinds of folks who would take his jibes lying low. Folks like Cara and Gibson Reynolds, a married dwarf couple from New Jersey, have attained celebrity status thanks to their adventures in the media spotlight. Here's what happened.

In 2006, the Reynolds's gave an interview to the *Associated Press* (AP) for an article about whether it was right to allow parents to create "perfect" babies. The Reynolds couple claimed that they had the right to do so. "You cannot tell me that I cannot have a child who's going to look like me," they reportedly said.

Then enter McHale, the irreverent host of *The Soup*, an E! Entertainment TV weekly show, which runs clips of what it considers the most notable pop culture and TV moments of each week. In a 2009 clip on the show, McHale ran an ad for a fake reality show to be called *Fertile Little Tattooed Pageant Parents Who Enjoy Baking*. Calling it the newest reality show, McHale showed the *Associated Press* photo of the Reynolds couple holding hands on their front porch and went ahead to describe them as "happy dwarves...that can't stop procreating." Then to illustrate his fake reality show, McHale altered the *AP* photo of the Reynolds couple to include images of babies with tattoos and wearing lingerie over their clothing.

The whole thing got the Reynolds's hopping mad, and they responded by filing a lawsuit in Philadelphia against pretty much everyone connected with the show: McHale himself, the television channel E! and Comcast, which owns E! In the lawsuit, the Reynolds couple sought more than $50,000 in damages for defamation and invasion of privacy. Mrs. Reynolds claimed that the piece, which allegedly also showed a woman purported to be her in labor in the bathroom giving birth, was so upsetting to her that she suffered "depression, insomnia, upset stomach, sleep interference, and feelings of shame and degradation."

For their part, the lawyers on McHale side are saying that the Reynolds' clip was just a "parody" which is protected by the First Amendment and nothing more than that.

So, what exactly is the deal here? Is this defamation or parody? Well, it depends!

First off, thanks to the First Amendment, America is any comedian's best home on earth and the reasons are obvious. Considering that Americans file more lawsuits than any other people on earth, the First Amendment clearly emerges as a comedian's best friend as well as his shield against what is perhaps the most obvious threat he faces on his job: a defamation lawsuit by people who have been rubbed the wrong way by something the comedian has said or done. To be sure, rubbing people the wrong way just goes with the comedian's territory. And as one might expect, McHale is already leaning so heavily on the First Amendment to save himself from the wrath of the Reynolds couple.

For better or worse, making fun of people the way McHale has done with the Reynolds couple just so happens to be something the law permits. Parody is one of the big things protected by the First Amendment. And whenever lawyers think about these kinds of situations, one of the more unforgettable cases they remember is the one where the Reverend Jerry Falwell sued the pornographer Larry Flynt and his *Hustler* magazine for $45 million over the cartoon piece where Falwell was portrayed as being drunk and having sex with his mother.

Despite the reverend's bitter objections, the U.S. Supreme Court in February 1988 said the cartoon piece was okay as a "parody" protected by the First Amendment. To be sure, the Supreme Court itself found the cartoon piece to be pretty offensive and this had to one of those cases where the Supreme Court literally held its nose with one hand and, metaphorically speaking, used the free hand to wave across a smelly cargo that is stinking up the whole place. The simple reason is that the First Amendment sets for itself the goal of promoting a "free marketplace of ideas," including, of course, humor. And we are talking mostly about the "public sphere" here.

So far, from the way the lawyers are talking in this case, a big part of this case will come down to whether the Reynolds's can be regarded as "public figures." A person can become a public figure by seeking the limelight and becoming a celebrity like Kim Kardashian. The other way someone can become a public figure is more by sheer accident, the way it happened with Captain Chesley "Sully" Sullenberger, the pilot who saved so many lives by landing that troubled US Airways plane on the Hudson River in New York City back in January 2009. But by whichever way any person gets to become a public figure, there are consequences for that status under the First Amendment, which include attracting the attention of saucy comedians and maybe receiving some pretty unwelcome ribbing from them.

In this very case, if the Reynolds couple can be regarded as "public figures," then it will become harder for them to overcome the idea that what McHale did was just a parody of life and events in society. Quite simply, the more Cara and Gibson Reynolds look like public figures, the weaker their case becomes. One thing is for sure, though: As far as public figures go, it may not be so easy to regard a couple like the Reynolds's as regular private citizens anymore, considering that they have made such gutsy remarks about creating "designer" babies, which seems kind of controversial, and perhaps even ahead of the times. To put it differently, it might be fair to say that because of their bold foray into the media arena, the Reynolds couple is no longer as anonymous as, say, the grocery store owner on the street corner. Especially not when they got involved with a renowned media organization like the Associated Press on a matter of public interest and (get this!) accompanied by the couple's photo. So, could it be said that the Reynolds's already injected themselves into the public space? Well, that's a question for the court.

But wait, there's something else. The Reynolds's lawsuit also contains an invasion of privacy claim against McHale and his co-defendants. Yet, any claim that McHale and his cohorts either invaded the seclusion of the Reynolds's (or perhaps exposed private facts about the Reynolds couple to the public) will most likely run into the same problem as the defamation claim. As it is, this is not like the typical invasion of privacy cases, such as the egregious ones where media organizations, without proper authorization, published photos of one woman nursing a child and of another laying nude in a bathtub. (In comparison to the nursing and bathtub photo cases, the Reynolds's situation is probably more like the photo of a couple kissing on a park bench.) Thus, to the contrary, it seems like the Reynolds's were already in the media limelight at the time McHale's side took a shot at them—McHale didn't have to pull back any curtains in order to find the Reynolds's. So, it was certainly the prerogative of the Reynolds couple to be controversial, but controversy also brings publicity and with it the attention of comedians.

Still, there is more to this case than just the folks involved, plus winning or losing this kind of case is something that would affect more than just the people who are in court here spending money on lawyers. For instance, if the Reynolds couple wins, going forward it could become dicey to make jokes about what someone else is doing or saying for fear that the joke might rub that person the wrong way. In other words, "parody" as we now know it won't be the same again. Needless to say, such a win will be an awesome thing for the Reynolds couple and other people who have been pissed off by jokes made by comedians.

But not so fast! The First Amendment stands in their way and their odds of winning seem rather long, at least longer than they are for comedians like McHale. For starters, attempting to punish somebody for making a satire of actual events in the life of society isn't exactly the best way for the First Amendment to promote a "free marketplace of ideas." So, perhaps it happens that what the Reynolds couple is looking for in this lawsuit may not be the kind of thing that the First Amendment stands for or would be eager to approve. (Jerry Falwell learned this bitter lesson when he sued Larry Flynt.)

In the end, no matter how this case turns out for the Reynolds couple, one thing is for sure: Life in a free speech society like America can be a bitch sometimes, because of all the [offensive] things that the law allows other people to be able to say and never get punished for. Yet, on the flip side, the Reynolds couple will have made their point at least: McHale and his people pissed them off and the couple dragged Team McHale into court and made them sweat the stuff. Talk about "messing with the wrong marine!"

THE WHEELCHAIR COMEDIAN: Between the Jailhouse and Free Speech

Ohio
July 10, 2012

The weird world of comedy can be a haven for both big laughs and the occasional puzzle. As things stand, not many people would guess that a crippled comedian in a wheelchair making fun of her disability in a public park would be told she may be breaking the law, or that folks helping her to promote her show at the park could go to jail for disorderly conduct. But that's exactly what happened at a park in Ohio this past May when Ally Bruener, a comedian with muscular dystrophy and her promoter-friend Forest Thomer went to a park in Cincinnati, Ohio, to promote her next gig and to steer visitors to her website. With Bruener sitting in a wheelchair at his side, Thomer reportedly went up to a group of folks at an event called "Party at the Park" and asked them if they wanted "to laugh at the crippled girl." After Thomer said that Bruener then told the group a joke as well as the place where she'd be performing her next gig plus her website address.

But apparently the officials at the park were in no mood for jokes and didn't find the whole thing funny. Soon, Cincinnati police were called and Thomer was arrested and charged with disorderly conduct. He could go to jail for thirty days if the charges against him stick. It is not entirely clear who said what to whom since some of the facts are still in dispute. An official at the park claimed that Thomer and Bruener did not walk away when they were asked to move on, but the comedy duo said that cops refused to tell them why Thomer was being arrested. Bruener and Thomer claim that the arrest of Thomer by the police amounts to a violation of their First Amendment free speech rights, especially their right to promote their comedy. "The police are trying to censor us. They're trying to tell us how we can or can't promote my comedy," Bruener said.

Well, there we go again, another day another free speech case. And to be sure, we are indeed in classic free speech territory since we are talking about an activity at a public park and the actions of the police. But aside from the back story as to why Thomer was arrested, the case perhaps is really about when a comic can advertise a gig in a public space such as a park without running afoul of the law. The other way to put this question is to ask how far the government can go in restricting the ability of comedians to promote their gigs at public spaces. And as long as we are talking about free speech and public spaces here, it has to be said that the freedom to promote a comedy event is no different from the freedom to promote any other kind of event, say, a rodeo or perhaps a ballgame.

So, how far can the government and its agents, such as the police, go in restricting the right of Americans, including comedians, to exercise their right to free speech by promoting their events, goods, or services at public places? Well, let's see what the law on free speech says. For starters, it is important to recognize that a public park represents what is called a "traditional public forum" where the constitution allows the biggest leeway for free speech. To put it in layman terms, a traditional public forum is pretty much the kind of place where folks can expect each other to 'swing their arms' as widely as they choose to swing them so long as their arms don't hit the next person who has the same right to do so. A public street or sidewalk would be another great example of a traditional public forum. At the other end of the spectrum are "non-public forums" run by the government, such as prisons or military bases, where the right to free speech is much more limited.

At a public forum like a public park, the kind of restriction that the government can put on speech depends on whether that speech is what is called "political speech or non-commercial speech," or whether the speech in question is "commercial speech or advertising." In short, if the speech is about advertising a product or service for sale, then it is commercial speech and it enjoys less protection than political speech. A political speech is pretty much any speech that is not advertising a product or service. Political speech receives the greatest protection by the law, especially if they are connected to a discussion or debate about public affairs. When we talk about "protecting" speech in this area, what we mean is that for the government to restrict a "political speech", the government has to show what the law calls a "compelling state interest."

This is another way of saying that the government has to show that there is pretty much no other way to protect or serve the public interest than to restrict the speech in question. A good example here would be a case where the police move in to stop a guy whose fiery speech at a public park would likely rile up folks to engage in violence and cause a disturbance of the peace. In that kind of situation, the "compelling state interest" could be that the government is trying to prevent a breakdown of law and order. Aside from these kinds of situations, the police cannot stop somebody from speaking at a public park just because the police don't like the person's views or philosophies, or even that the police would rather give the platform to another speaker with a different viewpoint. Choosing between speakers in this manner is no business of the police in a free speech nation and the law certainly doesn't permit that.

But while the government cannot restrict speech in a public park based on the speaker's views, it can however impose some restrictions as to the time, place, and manner in which the speeches can be made. And when dealing with advertising or commercial speech, the government does not have to show a "compelling state interest" in order to restrict advertising. In such a case, all that the government needs to be able to show is that the restriction it is trying to impose is a "reasonable" way to achieve its goals, and also that such restriction does not discriminate between one advertisement and another. Because advertisements or commercial speech enjoys "less protection" under free speech law, there is no need for the government to show that the restriction it is trying to impose is the only way to protect the public interest.

Then again, sometimes it may happen that the speech in question is a little bit of both advertising and political speech. One good example here might be a case where an ad is offering to provide abortion services at a family planning clinic for a fee. In this situation, one can say that the push to give women the freedom to receive abortion services is the political side of the equation, while the offer to charge a fee for rendering the service would fall on the commercial side of the equation. With such cases, because the package also contains political speech, which carries higher protection, the whole case would likely be treated as though we are dealing only with political speech. And so, the burden on the government will be higher when it attempts to restrict such speech.

So, what's the deal here and what does all this stuff mean for our case with the comedian in a wheelchair? Well, on the face of it, this may sound like a case where both advertising and political speech are in the mix. First of all, since the crippled comedian Bruener and her friend were trying to promote her gig at the park, we can safely suppose that the whole thing starts out as an advertisement or commercial speech. But the matter does not end there since it also appears that Bruener is trying to use the occasion to make a political statement about her disability. She claims she's using her comedy to break down a stigma in society, which considers crippled people as having a mental deficiency. "I want to open the door to the conversation...people don't expect the crippled girl to talk about it. When I bring it to light, it makes me more comfortable," Bruener said.

As already noted above, cases of this nature receive the kind of higher protection usually reserved for political speech. This basically means that in order to keep the wheelchair comedian and her friend out of the park in Cincinnati where they were promoting her gig, the government will be required to identify exactly what public interest it is serving by barring them from the park. Also, the government will be required to show that kicking the comedy duo out of the park is the only way to promote or serve that public interest. Obviously, this would be a tall mountain for the government to climb. Translation: the odds are mostly in favor of the crippled comic Bruener and her sidekick.

Yet, the government can still win the case if it can show that the crippled comedian and her sidekick violated some restrictions that exist at the park, such as perhaps rules adopted at the park which specifies the time, place, or manner of promoting events at the park. Usually, the government is allowed to impose such restrictions as long as they apply them to everyone using the park regardless of their views or opinions. If, for instance, the crippled comic and her friend walked into people or shouted obscenities at other park users or did other things that would cause undue annoyance to other users of the park, then they may be violating some time, place, and manner restrictions which are imposed on every user of the park. (For whatever it is worth to them, it is interesting to notice that the police have reportedly already made these kinds of allegations as part of their case against Thomer.)

One more thing: since we are dealing with the freedom of comedians to advertise their shows, it needs to be said that even if the comedy duo were not in a public park or on the streets, and even if the ad doesn't involve any political speech at all, it will still not be OK for the government to allow ads from other promoters but refuse to take ads from comedians. Such discrimination will be rejected as "unreasonable" under free speech law, except, of course, if the comedians' ads happen to be misleading, false, or deceptive or would promote unlawful activities. To be sure, this is the same test that is adopted for every other ad, whether it's an ad about comedy or not.

In the end, comedians do enjoy a lot of leeway when they get onstage to do their shtick. But before they arrive onstage, they are bound by the same rules of promoting gigs as other citizens, no more, no less. They cannot be subjected to more restrictions than others just because they are comedians and vice versa.

CASE UPDATE: On February 3, 2015, the City of Cincinnati settled the case for $25,000 in favor of Forest Thomer. This was to make way for the dismissal of his lawsuit against the city in federal court, in which he alleged a violation of his free speech rights in addition to a malicious prosecution claim. (The city had filed 'disorderly conduct' charges against him in state court in May 2012. After being acquitted by the state court of the city's charges against him, Thomer then launched his own case against the city in federal court, as described above.) As part of the settlement, the City of Cincinnati, as frequently happens in these situations, did not admit to any wrongdoing. In any event, it was obvious that everyone involved came to acknowledge that Thomer was acting within his constitutional rights and therefore never should have been arrested in the first place. Let's just say that the City of Cincinnati blinked on this one.

THE PREDICAMENT OF MIKE WARD: An American Perspective on Canadian Comedy

Canada
April 7, 2020

What's the difference between a Canadian comic and his American counterpart? Simple answer: location, location, location.

The brash Canadian comedian Mike Ward has had quite the unpleasant experience in his march through the comedy landscape of his country. From all indications, if he thought his native Canada was a place where a comedian could safely ply controversial material, he may just have figured wrong, it seems. And, for good measure, such a comedian could also find himself in the poor house should some in his audience decide to take him before the authorities.

But before getting into how Canadian and American comedy stack up against one another, it may be well to briefly recount the Mike Ward story:

In 2010, Ward, in a series of routines he performed at his shows in Canada, attacked a disabled kid named Jeremy Gabriel, whom he denounced as "ugly" and lamented the fact that the kid had not yet died. (Gabriel, thirteen years old at the time, was born with a condition known as Treacher Collins syndrome that left him with a deformed face and skull. At the time of Ward's verbal attack, Gabriel had become something of a local celebrity in Canada's Quebec province for his singing ability, including singing with Celine Dion, as well as singing for the Pope in 2006. Ward claimed that he had initially supported Gabriel's good fortune, on the assumption that the world was coddling him because he would soon die. Ward said that he felt duped when years had passed, and Gabriel was still going strong with his singing fame. In reaction, the comedian said he went on the Internet to find out exactly what

Gabriel was suffering from. Ward said he was surprised at what he discovered: "You know what it was? He's ugly, godammit!"

Well, Gabriel and his family sued Ward before the Quebec Human Rights Commission for allegedly "hurting, vexing, and humiliating" him as well as for damaging his (Gabriel's) confidence and singing career and causing him to be mocked at school. In its 2016 ruling, the commission said that the comedian's joke violated Gabriel's right to dignity, honor, and reputation as well as his right to equality and to be safe from discrimination. As a remedy, it penalized Ward with a total fine of $42,000 (consisting of $35,000 to Gabriel himself and $7,000 to his mom).

The commission's ruling outraged Ward and many of his supporters in the comedy community. He promptly set up a crowdfunding campaign and launched an appeal against the ruling. Speaking on behalf of other comics, Ward said: "If the judgment is maintained, no one will be able to dare to be a stand-up comic, because normally you make fun of things that are controversial, otherwise it's not funny. ...If anything, that's controversial can authorize someone to say, I was hurt, I'm going to court, then we're finished." Then he tagged on an interesting analogy: "To bring a comedian to court who does dark humor, for a trashy joke, is like giving Vin Diesel a speeding ticket for driving fast in [the movie] *The Fast and the Furious*."

Now, let's consider a different scenario, this time involving Canada and the U.S., its close neighbor to the south. Both countries are democracies and open societies. So, suppose the Ward situation occurred in the U.S., will the comedian's fate be any different? In other words, if Ward would have appeared at some comedy venue in America and viciously attacked some disabled kid, will he face a peril to his career similar to what happened to him in Canada? Well, the short answer is: Probably not!

For starters, considering the central role of the First Amendment's free speech guarantee in the conversation in America's public square, there would seem to be no room for an agency like the Quebec Human Rights Commission. In fact, the agency's watchdog role carries way too much potential for censorship than America's First Amendment could even live with. To the blessing of comedians in America, controversial speech oddly seems to enjoy enormous protection from censorship. To say things that hurt somebody else's feelings or even things that are very cruel are allowed in America's social conversation. Needless to say, Americans get it clearly that the "free society" they pride themselves in can also be a pretty uncomfortable society where some of the most offensive things ever may yet be safely said. Pretty much everything is allowed, other than a few situations like where somebody's speech could be viewed as obscene, or as inciting violence or be considered as "fighting words" (the sort that would likely draw a violent reaction from the person to whom they are addressed).

So, in the above scenario, merely attacking a disabled kid, however viciously and however tacky the action might seem, would not be reason enough to find legal liability against an American comedian, and thus to impose a punishing fine upon him. In short, the Mike Ward ordeal is simply a Canadian story that is hard to imagine in a place like America.

However, given the Gabriel family's other allegation that Ward damaged Gabriel's reputation by his joke, plus the commission's references to Gabriel's honor and reputation in its decision, some have wondered why a good old-fashioned defamation action cannot be successfully pursued against Ward even in an American court. Well, not much luck here, either. And the reason is simple enough: Statements that a professional funnyman made to audiences who understood said statements as a joke would not qualify as the kind of false statement of fact that would damage somebody else's reputation, which is the very point of a defamation action.

Yet just because comedians south of the border are allowed by the law to be offensive to others doesn't mean that an American comedian whose stock in trade is the plying of unnecessarily "outrageous" material will enjoy a smooth sail to a comfortable career. In an era of political correctness and cancel culture, there is the law and then there is the court of public opinion, two different venues. Whereas the law may not take an outrageous comedian's money from him by way of court fines, the consuming public, for its part, may refuse to give him any money at all by simply not patronizing his comedy. This is a powerful reality that neither Ward nor any comedian in America or Canada for that matter can afford to ignore.

Still, in America, fortunately for comics, political correctness and the law continue to have some good degree of separation from each other, unlike in Canada where they currently appear to the merging, and this surely can't be good news for comedy. As the Mike Ward situation demonstrates, it seems that when speaking of the very survival of a comedian's career, dealing with the whims of political correctness and cancel culture are more manageable hazards than the blunt instrument of a court order directed at the comedian. To be sure, an unfavorable court order is no laughing matter, even for a funnyman.

GOING TO JAIL FOR A JOKE: A Contemporary American Look at German Comedy

Germany
March 12, 2017

The saying that America is a free country is something that Americans in the comedy business in contemporary times would probably appreciate better than most people. But in other places, however, thanks to their laws, comedians live in a different world and in some cases can actually go to jail for the content of their comedy. Perhaps surprisingly, Germany seems to be one of those places.

Take the case of comedian Jan Bohmermann. In March 2016, Bohmermann, a German insult comedian and host of the satirical talk show *Neo Magazine Royale* took an offensive shot at Turkish leader Recep Tayyip Erdogan. Sitting in front of a Turkish flag and a portrait of Erdogan, Bohmermann read a poem in which he suggested, among other things, that the Turkish leader had sex with goats and watched child porn. Perhaps this was great comedy for his audience, but the offensive gag did in fact run up against an actual law in Germany that forbids anyone from insulting a foreign leader. The punishment? Up to three years jail or a fine.

Not surprisingly, the reaction of the Turkish government was swift and harsh. In demanding that Bohmermann be immediately punished for his action, the Turkish government denounced the satirical poem as a "serious crime against humanity...that crossed all lines of indecency" as well as an insult to all Turkish people's honor. For her part, German chancellor Angela Merkel (under pressure to preserve her country's refugee deal and its overall fragile relations with Turkey) also condemned the poem as "deliberately offending," and noted that Germany's freedom of the media was not an unlimited right. Sensing that it had stepped into it, Germany's ZDF, the public broadcaster that carries the

107

comedian's talk show, yanked the video from its website as well as on YouTube.

In contemporary America, it's taken for granted that something like the Bohmermann situation cannot happen here, and indeed that is true. Thanks to the First Amendment's prescription for "uninhibited, robust, and wide-open" debate on matters of public concern, it's difficult to imagine any situation where a contemporary American comedian can be arrested and charged in a similar manner for the content of their comedy. (Of course, there are a few well-understood exceptions to free speech rights.) Usually, if it should happen that some foreign leader doesn't like a particular joke made by some American comedian, well, tough luck! No wonder it is said that the First Amendment is the comedian's best friend, and that America is the freest place on earth where a person can do comedy, gadflies like Bohmermann included.

Yet, in perspective, the American cultural landscape wasn't always such a danger-free zone for any comedian who would push the envelope and thereby ruffle neatly arranged feathers or step on sensitive toes. The legendary American comedian Lenny Bruce is remembered as much for his heroic advocacy of free speech as for the tragic price he paid for doing so. Bruce was the classic iconoclast who never hesitated to attack the conventions of the American society of his time in a bid to expose what he considered as their hypocrisy, whether the conventions concerned religion, sexuality, race, the flag, and more. Consequently, between 1961 and 1964, he was arrested for obscenity in places like San Francisco, Los Angeles, Chicago, and New York. The encounter in New York ended in an actual criminal conviction. (By the time he died in August 1966 of a drug overdose, his conviction was yet to be overturned on appeal. He was finally pardoned in 2003 by the governor of New York.) Today, thanks to Lenny Bruce and his leadership in the free speech battles of his era, no American comedian since then has been charged with a crime for the content of their comedy.

Speaking of Bohmermann, this past fall, the German authorities who had been weighing an indictment against him opted not to do so, citing lack of evidence. For what it's worth, they claimed that since Bohmermann's crude poem was simply an example of what would constitute overstepping the boundaries of freedom of opinion rather than him actually expressing his own views about Erdogan, he didn't violate the law after all. In other words, whatever Bohmermann was doing with his poem was OK as long as he had not expressed his own personal opinion about Erdogan.

Now, for anyone who really cares about free expression, the trouble with this kind of reasoning is that Bohmermann was saved from going to jail precisely because he did not in fact (allegedly) express his own personal views about the subject he was dealing with. Translation: as German law sees it, not saying what is on one's mind is actually the way to avoid trouble and jail. Really? Well, let's just say that Americans, whether they are comedians or not, simply do not see freedom of expression in this way.

The other intriguing fact here is how even Bohmermann himself perhaps seems not to quite grasp the deeper implication of the prosecutor's decision. To be sure, he was right (as a free speech advocate) in railing against the authorities for launching the investigation at all as well as for stating that "if a joke triggers a state crisis, it is not the problem of the joke, but of the state." Only problem is, Bohmermann would have to be living in a place like America where that kind of protection exists as a fact of life for comedians, courtesy of the First Amendment. Given the way things actually work in Germany where he lives, it is obvious that as long as this particular law remains unchanged, a joke which triggers a state crisis could indeed land a comedian in jail if that joke happens to be his personal opinion on the subject. Especially when such a joke rubs prickly foreign leaders like Erdogan the wrong way. Not a happy picture!

Still, it isn't all fun and games in American comedy today and indeed may not be so any time soon. Although nothing quite compares to going to jail for doing a comedy act, as it was in the Lenny Bruce era, it remains true that the current culture of political correctness does present quite a headwind for the flourishing of American comedy. Where a comedian in the 1960s would have worried about a cop in the audience arresting him for, say, obscenity, today's comedians instead worry about their act offending the so-called "PC police" on social media and other forums in the public square. Incidentally, the growing clout of the PC police has caused some famed contemporary comedians like Jerry Seinfeld and Chris Rock to opt to skip doing shows on college campuses where being politically correct seems now to be almost a religion. However, to America's advantage in the America vs. Germany match-up, we're really talking about the impact of an actual penal law versus a mere social phenomenon that comedians, admittedly, find unpleasant. A night and day difference, it seems. Besides, it's not as though German comedians themselves also don't have to worry about being politically correct, just like the Americans. They actually do! Not least because Germany for all its free speech deficiencies is still (get this!) another western society and an advanced democracy that exists in the 21st century.

In the end, the Bohmermann situation in Germany is something that really ought to be a big deal whenever an American comedian counts his or her blessings. For although the impact of PC may seem like a "rain on the parade" for American comedians, it is still safe to say that compared to other places, including similar western societies like Germany, doing comedy in contemporary America is a great experience like no other. As they say, it's a free country, live in it! And bring the comedy with you!

PROMOTING COMEDY EVENTS IN THE PUBLIC FORUM: Learning the Tricky Ropes

United States
August 25, 2021

As democracies go, America is a haven for the practice of comedy, thanks to the First Amendment, which protects the right of free speech. And, in this area, public forums are very important, especially those venues provided by the government, which are often the venues with the largest audiences for many a speaker. However, access to those venues is neither as free nor as guaranteed by law as the right to free speech itself. Indeed, often times people erroneously assume that easy access to a public forum is just something of a matter of course. Wrong!

On closer examination, a lot of folks, comedians included, have been surprised to find that there are quite a bit of rules or regulations (principles, if you will) that govern someone's right of access to speak at a public forum.

By the way, comedians might be interested to note here that *speech* in this context includes not just things that are said at an actual show, but also things that are written or said in the process of advertising a show or event, say, on billboards or posters.

As a general rule, what one can say on a particular public forum depends on what sort of forum the place is, namely, whether it is a traditional public forum or a "designated" or limited public forum. With traditional public forums, such as public parks and street corners, life is easy and you can think of those places as free speech highways where all manner of speech is allowed, both political and ideological, and non-political speech, which includes commercial speech like advertising and the like. In these forums, the government cannot restrict or deny speech based on the "content" of that speech, meaning, for instance, that it cannot decide to allow commercial speech but ban religious speech. Nope!

In order for the government to do so, it must show not only that it had a "compelling" interest or reason for restricting or denying speech, but also that it had no other means available to it to achieve the same result in a manner that would have had less impact on the speech in question. Lawyers call this the "strict scrutiny" rule, the whole point of which is to make it very difficult for the government to mess around with any of the "protected" rights under the constitution. (Note that although the government isn't allowed to ban or restrict any constitutionally "protected" speech it is nevertheless allowed to regulate the time, place and manner of exercising the right.)

Then there are the "designated" or limited public forums, such as subways and buses, which are places where the government can choose what sort of speech to allow and which ones to prohibit. Government can choose, for instance, to ban political speech while allowing commercial speech. But as long as it has opted to allow commercial speech, it cannot then start to discriminate between commercial speeches on the basis of "viewpoint." In other words, the government's actions in restricting or denying speech in such situations must be "viewpoint- neutral and reasonable," meaning that it cannot, for example, treat similar speeches differently.

For comedians and other entertainers who frequently need to publicize their shows in the public forum, the limited public forums are the ones that appear to raise the trickiest questions.

In the ordinary case, an ad by, say, a computer store on a city bus is a straightforward business promotion and often goes off without a hitch. However, problems might arise where what is said in an ad, for instance, can be perceived as "political" in nature and/ or controversial and thus banned. And this is where comedians can sometimes run into unexpected difficulties with exercising their free speech in such public forums.

Perhaps one of the more interesting cases here is the one involving some Muslim comedians who in September 2014 wanted to advertise their documentary film *The Muslims Are Coming* through the use of posters in the New York City subway system operated by the Metropolitan Transit Authority (MTA). The said movie, produced one year earlier, follows some Muslim-American comedians on their tour of American towns and cities and their interactions with the audiences.

The various poster ads contained the link to the movie's website as well as various comic statements, including things like "Muslims Hate Terrorists;" "They also hate;" "People who tell you they went to an Ivy League School within 10 seconds of meeting them;" "When the deli guy doesn't put enough schmear on the bagel;" and "Getting out that last bit of toothpaste from the tube." The ads also contained statements like "Those Terrorists are all Muslim [the word "Muslim" is crossed out] Nutjobs," "Grown up Muslims can do more pushups than baby Muslims" and so on. The six ads were scheduled to run over a one-month period in 144 ads across the city's subways. But the MTA rejected the proposed ads on the grounds that the ads violated its newly adopted policy, which allowed commercial speech while barring the use of its facilities for "political" speech.

However, the comedians Dean Obeidallah and Negin Farsad plus the ad's producer Vaguely Qualified Productions sued the MTA and got a big win in federal court. In siding with the comedians, the court ruled instead that the ads were essentially "commercial" speech by a for-profit entity and that it remained so even if the advertiser might have been trying to capitalize on the political controversy around Islamophobia to promote its business interest. (At the time in question, the right-wing activist Pamela Geller's group the American Freedom Defense Initiative [AFDI] was reportedly running an anti-Muslim ad in the said subways, depicting a man in a headscarf with the addition of the incendiary words "Killing Jews Is Worship That Draws Us Close to Allah." The Muslim comedians claimed they were simply trying to counter the possible cultural impact of that campaign.)

Furthermore, the court said that even if the ads could be considered as "political" speech, the MTA had engaged in "viewpoint discrimination" given that it had already allowed other ads on its platform that were arguably even more political in nature than the comedians' ads in this case: cable TV station CNN's ran its ad about the GOP presidential debate, which contained photos and quotes by the candidates. In other words, the court found that the MTA, which offered its subways and buses as a limited public forum for speech, was treating similar things differently in violation of the principle of "viewpoint-neutrality."

What are some of the lessons here? For starters, the less political speech contained in ads for a show, the easier life will be for the comedian. Obviously, things can get tricky when the ads straddle the political and the commercial lanes of traffic: in such situations, the authorities might be tempted to use the excuse of stopping political speech to perhaps ban the ads of a rather controversial comedian they might not like. (This is arguably what the MTA was trying to do in the Muslim comedians' case, as the court implied.) The other thing is that when it comes to ads and free speech, life is easiest in classic public forums like public parks and streets where the test is "strict scrutiny" (meaning the government must clear a very high hurdle before it can restrict the ads). Also, note that things can get a little hard in limited public forums like subways and buses, and even harder in nonpublic forums like public schools, public hospitals or even jail houses.

With all that in mind, the good news, though, is that even in the forums that are less friendly to free speech, such as the limited public forums or totally nonpublic forums, there is still the protection of the First Amendment, which requires that there be no viewpoint discrimination. In any event, ads containing statements or images that might be considered as "obscene" or statements that amount to "fighting words" or which could be viewed as "incitement to violence" are not protected under the First Amendment regardless of the forum involved.

COPYING THE WORK
OR APPEARANCE OF
SOMEBODY ELSE

CHAPTER THREE

COPYING THE WORK OR APPEARANCE OF SOMEBODY ELSE

In the last chapter, we dealt with situations that show how the law protects the right of comedians to speak freely about people or things generally and, if they choose, to knock somebody else, or for that matter to knock something that the comedians feel should perhaps get such treatment. Many of those cases, as we saw, are the defamation cases where the First Amendment really comes into play, especially when we're talking about people in the public eye. However, there are other situations where the comedian may not be knocking somebody else but instead is accused of copying somebody else's work or perhaps trying to make-believe that they are that other person. So then, what happens when somebody is claiming that some comedian is causing harm to them by copying their work or when a comedy-oriented business is claiming that some rival business operation is harming them by passing themselves off in the marketplace as the business of the person complaining?

The cases in this section address just those kinds of disputes. Whether we're talking about the allegations against Fox TV's hit sitcom *Glee* or Comedy Central's animated show *South Park* or

The Hangover movie , one thing is clear: in the business world, serious money is often at stake in these kinds of situations, and they're certainly no laughing matter. Well, speaking of how courts handle these situations, it's fair to say that when somebody is selling comedy out there in the business world, they are held to the same standards as other players in the business landscape, especially when it comes to the rules of fair competition. So now, the cases . . .

* * *

GLEE! SEE YOU IN COURT: Trouble from Across the Pond

Britain
April 9, 2012

As success sometimes brings trouble, so goes the story of the Fox hit comedy *GLEE*, a big-money show that is loved by so many on both sides of the Atlantic. This time the trouble is all in the show's name itself: *Glee*. As it happens, not everyone thinks the hit musical show, which is a Golden Globe winner with about eleven soundtrack albums, plays by fair rules or should even be allowed to continue to run on TV. Across the pond, the British comedy company, Comic Enterprises, which runs a chain of music and comedy venues in Britain called the *Glee Club*, is suing Twentieth Century Fox for trademark infringement, claiming that the use of the name *Glee* by the American TV show is causing its customers to think there is a link between the British club and the American sitcom; it further claims that the confusion is damaging its business. Fox has responded to the British lawsuit with a counterclaim of its own, challenging the right of the British comedy company to own the "Glee" name.

In a typical trademark infringement case, the goal is pretty much to collect money from the person causing the offense and often times to shut down the business operation or practice altogether. And that is what makes this case such a big deal: Although Glee is now listed among the top ten digital US albums of all time, the British market is also a gold mine for the American hit show and its fortunes in Britain run into "tens of millions of pounds." Last year's concert tour by the cast of *Glee* sold more than 165,000 tickets in Britain. A win for the British comedy company will mean they could get paid millions of dollars plus an injunction or court order that would either yank the entire TV show or force its creators to change the show as we presently know it in the British market. Not a pretty thing!

With the stakes so high, what are the odds of Comic Enterprises winning the case? Not that bad, really! Well, let's look at the law of trademark infringement. First of all, the whole point of having a "trademark", whether it's in the form of a word, a design or something else, is to identify the "source" of goods or services in the marketplace through differentiating one person's goods or services from those of other suppliers. This is really about branding and avoiding "confusion" of one supplier's product for those of other suppliers. And, as one might expect, suppliers who have built up a lot of "goodwill" in their product or service over the years would be especially keen to protect their trademark.

So, to win a trademark infringement case, the person bringing the claim has to actually show that they in fact own the "mark" in question, and that the other person or supplier who is getting sued is using that same mark, or perhaps a mark so similar to it that it would likely cause confusion in the minds of consumers out there in the marketplace. The plaintiff also needs to show that the offending supplier is using the mark in carrying on a business without having any permission or a valid defense for doing so.

So, for starters, if the people filing the suit cannot, in fact, show that they own the mark, then their claim would go nowhere and all the talk about customers getting confused or the other guy having no permission to use the mark won't even matter at all. And this is the one factor that could make or break our case here because Twentieth Century Fox seems to have pushed that question to center court by claiming that Comic Enterprises does not own the "Glee" trademark. If Fox can make this claim stick, that would be the end of the road for their opponents. But can it?

To prove that someone owns a trademark, registration of the mark with the appropriate authorities is perhaps the best way to show ownership of the mark against everyone else. Here, Comic Enterprises reportedly registered the Glee name for its clubs since

1999 in the sectors of entertainment services and even merchandise in Britain. And for good measure, the British market is the "marketplace" that really counts in this lawsuit, not the American or any other market for that matter.

Yet, registration alone simply doesn't cut it because an opponent can still challenge the validity of the mark, just as Fox has done. To knock out their opponent's claim, Fox is bringing the Oxford English Dictionary into court and checking out what it says about the word *glee*, which is that a glee club is a society for singing part-songs. In layman's language, Fox is pretty much saying that when the word *glee* is used, it's really more about people singing in a group, rather than something about a comedy club.

To be sure, the registration of a trademark offers a huge advantage to a party in any trademark lawsuit and Fox here is merely trying to do its best in a pretty difficult situation. Since we are talking about trademarks as things that distinguish goods and services from one another, it means that relying on words that merely describe or say what a business does may not be such a powerful argument after all. This is because, technically, any other supplier in that line of business could claim a right to use that same word and this sort of free riding is something the trademark law frowns upon. With Fox, this means that folks who are singing could use the word *glee* when referring to themselves.

To strengthen their position, somebody using commonplace words like *glee* or something else has, usually tries to demonstrate that the said word has in the course of time, acquired what is called a "secondary meaning," in that the average consumer in that particular market links or associates that particular word with that particular supplier.

Yet, the bigger odds in this lawsuit are that Fox will probably end up fighting its case on other grounds than just relying on the dictionary meaning of the word or trying to say that the registration is not valid. But the good news for Fox is that even if Comic Enterprises shows that its registration of the Glee name was valid, it still has to show that its customers are likely to be confused by associating the Fox TV show with the featured events of its business, the Glee Club. In other words, will the ordinary guy out there on the streets of Britain really think that the events of the Fox TV show and those of the Glee Club are coming to them from the same source? Proving that kind of stuff in the dust and smoke of a courtroom trial can get dicey in the real world.

In the end, this case likely won't be a walk in the park for either party. Given the high stakes in this case for Fox, such as the big money that its hit TV show is making in the British market, plus the risk of a negative court order, this is no laughing matter for Fox, and it will likely do all it can to make this matter go away. Predictions are hard to make in these kinds of cases, but Fox clearly seems to get the memo already: there's possible legal peril here and it probably wouldn't want a foreign judge deciding on matters like the kinds of circumstances which could possibly confuse British consumers in the marketplace, or for that matter what possible creative changes might become necessary for the show's survival in the foreign marketplace.

And there is already a danger signal from the courtroom: A judge in the case has warned that the TV show "at least in its current form would have to be taken off the air" if Fox loses. The way things are looking these days, the odds of an out-of-court settlement of this lawsuit have never been better.

CASE UPDATE: Well, in the end, Fox lost and was ordered to drop the Glee name in Britain.

On February 7, 2014, about three years after the lawsuit began, the [High] Court in Britain agreed with the plaintiff Comic Enterprises that the name "Glee" being used by the Fox TV show did in fact infringe upon the plaintiff's trademark rights to the phrase "The Glee Club," which is the name used by the plaintiff in running its comedy clubs in Britain. In response, a defiant Twentieth Century Fox vowed to appeal: "We intend to appeal and are confident that, as the case plays out, we will ultimately prevail...We remain committed to delivering *Glee* to all of its fans in the UK."

While the appeal was pending, the court agreed to hold off on ordering Twentieth-Century Fox to drop the TV show's name until the appeal was decided. Fox had told the court that being forced to change the name of the show for its British viewers would be disproportionate, costly and complex. In the end, Twentieth Century Fox lost the appeal, with the court agreeing that "the exists a likelihood of confusion." Accordingly, the *Glee* name was ordered to be dropped in the British market.

JOKE THEFT? *SNL's* Michael Che in the Cross Hairs

New York
January 7, 2022

There we go again with the joke-stealing thing: another accusation, another comedy star, another lawsuit. This time Michael Che's number is up in the plagiarism altercations of the internet age. In case you missed it, the *Saturday Night Live* (*SNL*) funnyman has been accused of purloining (okay, stealing) jokes from a TikTok video performer and now both Che and his partner HBO Max have been dragged to court. And the TikToker is asking for more than just money.

Kelly Manno is a TikTok performer who posts videos on the said platform covering various everyday situations like taking a home tour, grabbing fast food with kids in the car, carpools by moms and more. Last year around August and September, she released two TikTok videos, which she claimed garnered many hundreds of thousands of views. The videos titled the "Homegirl Hotline" involved a fictional service, which allows people to request a so-called "homegirl" to help them take care of personal problems in their lives. (In one of the TikTok skits, after being called in to help an upset woman get even with a cheating boyfriend, the assisting "homegirl" threw out the bad guy's clothing from the woman's upstairs window, then drops a label that reads "free shit" over the clothes strewn on the lawn downstairs before proceeding to puncture the tires of the guy's SUV truck that was packed downstairs.) Typically, after the "homegirl" deal is struck, the customer would express their gratitude by saying, "Thank You, Homegirl."

Enter Michael Che and his HBO Max comedy series titled *That Damn Michael Che*. One of the episodes of the series contains a sketch entitled "Homegrrl." There, a father's young son is attacked at a building lobby by an agitated woman who claims that the boy had stolen something from her and was hiding it in his diaper.

During the attack, another woman intervenes and punches out the woman who had lunged at the kid and then apologizes to the kid's flustered father who then replies, "Thanks, Homegrrl!" It is this very line uttered by this father character in Che's sketch that Manno claims infringes her copyright in the phrase "Thank You, Homegirl Hotline" which was uttered by the characters in her own video. So, in her lawsuit, Manno is alleging that Che has willfully infringed her copyright in the video and is seeking serious money damages plus a court order (or injunction) stopping Che and HBO from continuing to use their sketch.

Now let's consider what the copyright law says about all this. For starters, one cannot obtain copyright in a work unless the said work is an "original" work that has been affixed to a "tangible" medium. Obviously then, Manno's work here, whatever one might say of its quality, is "original" in nature (assuming, of course, that she didn't lift the stuff from somebody else). Plus, TikTok as a platform qualifies as a "tangible" medium where works being presented for copyright protection can be situated. Therefore, at first blush, Manno's "Homegirl Hotline" skit passes the copyright test and will be recognized as a "work" in which her copyright exists.

So, now that she's sitting pretty as a copyright holder, how about Che? Did he, in fact, infringe her copyright? Well, not if he came up with his own work entirely on his own, in which case we will be dealing with a mere coincidence (which is okay) rather than a willful appropriation, which is not allowed. And of course, if we're talking about willful infringement, we must assume that Che indeed had "access" to Manno's work. (For folks in Manno's position, one of the blessings of the Internet age is that proving "access" of this kind is a cakewalk because, hey, we all suppose that anyone can access anything posted for public consumption on a platform like TikTok.)

Setting aside the question of coincidence, could the two works each enjoy copyright protection despite their apparent similarity?

Well, yeah: one cannot copyright an idea but rather only the particular (i.e., original) way that the person has expressed the said idea. When we're dealing with words, as in this case, what is or can be protected, incidentally, is the very way the words have been used rather than the all-too-familiar idea of expressing gratitude to someone (whether Homegirl or anybody else) who has done the speaker a favor. Translation: Even if someone in Che's position saw the thing on the Internet, he can still avoid the copyright problem by simply using different words to express the same good-manners idea of gratitude. (Again, remember, no one can copyright an idea.) So, in the complicated world of copyright law, just proving that the second person had "access" to the first person's work isn't even enough. Between the issues of coincidence, access, and similarity of the works in question, the jury in these sorts of cases is dealing with and weighing up a lot of factors, which all makes for potentially expensive litigation and an oftentimes hard-to-predict outcome.

This case brings to mind another copyright situation from across the pond in Britain, a case that just like the Che's case, involves a lesser-known person going after someone with a higher public profile, as well as the same issues of coincidence, access, and the use of similar ideas and expressions. Only this time the dispute is between two actual working standup comedians, and funny enough, the dispute has led not to a copyright violation suit by the complaining comedian, but rather a defamation lawsuit by the comedian who allegedly stole the other guy's joke. (Feel free to call it the "smart fridge case," if you like.)

In the British case, both comedians are making a joke about not wanting to buy a smart fridge, out of fear that said fridge would actually bother them with messages when then they're away from home hanging out with their friends. One comedian (Darius Davies) claimed he first made the joke on the comedy club circuit prior to the second comedian (Kae Kurd) making the same joke on national TV. Kurd, whose time on TV with the joke seemed to have garnered him newfound celebrity status (a prestigious talent agency rep plus a national tour) did sue Davies for defamation for essentially calling him a joke thief in a viral post that aired the accusation.

Although Davies has not filed a countersuit for copyright infringement against Kurd, the circumstances that existed between them before Kurd went to court present the same old copyright issues of coincidence, access, and similarity of ideas/expression that we see in Che's case. Indeed, they'd already argued over these issues (without any resolution) prior to the matter landing in court. At the moment, the parties are reportedly taking the traditional path of trying to resolve matters out of court. Makes sense in the circumstances.

Returning to Michael Che's case, it seems that the British situation offers clues as to the likely path out of the dispute: an out of court settlement. For a comedy star like Che, it may not be the best use of time and money to be wrangling about possible joke theft with a lesser-known quantity like Manno. There's probably no path to a happy win for Che nor for HBO Max. If one were to take a bet, the odds are better than even that they'll choose to just settle this pesky matter out of court and be done with it. But we'll see how it all ends.

ACCUSING CONAN O'BRIEN, PART ONE: Two Joke Writers Walk into a Courtroom

California
November 10, 2015

Accusing people of joke stealing has become such an old problem in comedy that it hardly raises eyebrows anymore. Except maybe when somebody is actually accusing an industry heavyweight like Conan O'Brien of being, ahem, a joke thief. But this one case seems more interesting than most because of the rather contemporary feel to it all: the alleged joke heist took place on Twitter, the emerging "it" forum for pushing jokes in our social media age. So, behold an old problem invading a new space. Even though said problem is still an unresolved menace in all the old places it had come from. But first here's the story:

This past July, a comedy writer in the San Diego area named Robert Alex Kaseberg filed a copyright violation lawsuit in federal court in California against Conan O'Brien and all those associated with his show, including TBS, Time Warner, Inc., and his writing staff. Kaseberg alleged that four of his jokes, which he'd posted on his personal blog and on Twitter had subsequently appeared on O'Brien's monologue during his TBS late-night show *Conan* without any attribution to him or compensation to him. The four jokes at issue ranged from gags about Delta Airlines and Tom Brady to the Washington Monument and Bruce Jenner.

Here's a sample of some of the jokes allegedly stolen by O'Brien:

> *Kaseberg: "A Delta flight this week took off from Cleveland to New York with just two passengers and they fought over control of the armrest the entire flight."*
> *O'Brien: "On Monday, a Delta flight from Cleveland to New York took off with just two passengers. Yet somehow, they spent the whole flight fighting over the armrest."*

> *Kaseberg: "The Washington Monument is ten inches shorter than previously thought. You know the winter has been cold when a monument suffers from shrinkage."*
> O'Brien: "Surveyors announced that the Washington Monument is ten inches shorter than what's been recorded. Of course, the monument is blaming the shrinkage on the cold weather."

Anyhow, Kaseberg seeks hundreds of thousands of dollars in damages.

In the scheme of things, this case seems to have a bit more significance than many might think at first blush. For starters, it shows that the old worries about joke stealing in comedy won't be going away anytime soon; indeed, the problem has now migrated to the social media arena, as it tracks the movements of the modern comedian and the newfound location of comedy audiences today. Unlike comedy clubs, Twitter is more like an open access forum, where things like a cover charge, drink minimums or other similar restrictions do not exist.

The other angle to this story presents something of a David and Goliath scenario: like, when a lesser-known comedian is claiming the same joke as a nationally known late-night comedian with the large microphone of national TV, all the advantages seem to run in one direction so that the odds of the lesser-known guy (the little guy) winning that battle is usually pretty steep – and punishing. Assuming, of course, that the person who's being accused actually stole the joke from the other.

But anyhow, aside from who has a bigger microphone between the two, when we consider just the law, can the little guy in this case actually win? Well, let's see:

For starters, it is obvious from the present lawsuit that we're dealing here with copyright law. And although Twitter is a new medium, the idea of violating someone else's copyright—either in a joke or in some other protected things like a movie or a book—is still the same. In very simple terms, for a piece of work to receive copyright protection under the law, it is required to be both "original" as well as be fixed in a "tangible medium of expression." As the name implies, an "original" idea is something that the person claiming the copyright protection basically came up with on their own; in other words, something not copied from somebody else, so to speak. Well, there are some rules, perhaps many rules around the whole notion of "originality" in copyright law. For instance, certain things or ideas are just not of the kind that can be protected by copyright and so no one can be granted a copyright on them.

The oh-so-common expression "Happy Birthday!" for instance, probably falls into the class of expressions for which no one can be granted a copyright. Again, just because two people seem to have expressed their ideas in the same exact way doesn't necessarily mean that a copyright has been breached. In such a situation, it must also be shown that the person who is alleged to have violated the claimant's copyright actually had access to the said copyrighted material. Otherwise, the alleged similarity between the two works could possibly be chalked up to mere coincidence. Yeah, a showing of coincidence could actually save the day for the person being accused of copyright violation.

To return to the O'Brien situation, two things look like they are clear: first, the jokes being claimed by Kaseberg seem to be original enough as to qualify for copyright protection, assuming, of course, that he has properly registered those particular jokes at the Copyright Office; second, the jokes involved here were affixed to a tangible medium, namely, Twitter. Plus, it is also true that Kaseberg published the said jokes on Twitter before O'Brien used them in his monologues on his show. (The Delta flight joke, for instance, appeared on Kaseberg's Twitter page earlier in the day on January 14 before O'Brien made his own joke later that same day in his late-night monologue.)

But that's not the end of the matter. Among other things, even though Twitter is an open forum where anybody can have access to, Kaseberg will still have to show that O'Brien actually lifted the jokes from his Twitter page. Interestingly, O'Brien's people have already rejected the suggestion that they got the joke from Kaseberg's sources. In a reported conversation between Kaseberg and the *Conan* show's head writer Mike Sweeney (published on Kaseberg's blog), Sweeney did "angrily and loudly" deny that the jokes came from Kaseberg and was "furious" and "incensed" at the suggestion that his writers would have anything to do with the "pathetic blog of a no-name failure" like Kaseberg. Despite the striking similarity between the O'Brien and Kaseberg jokes, the obvious implication of the pretty hard pushback by O'Brien's side is the claim that his people (the writers on his show) came up with the jokes by themselves. Well, unless Kaseberg has some kind of smoking gun of the alleged heist, he doesn't seem to have a pathway to victory here. Plus, it doesn't help him too much that only the Delta flight joke comes up on a search of his blog or Twitter record from that period; the other three do not.

At this point, it is not clear how long this litigation will drag on and for that matter how well Kaseberg's claims will hold up in the end. If one were to take a bet on the outcome of the case, it would seem like a better bet to say that the case will settle somehow and not go the distance. Although Team O'Brien might well decide, standing on principle, to fight this whole thing to the bitter end, the odds of a settlement of this matter looks somewhat decent.

At this point, for O'Brien's side, the bigger pain isn't so much the merits of Kaseberg's lawsuit as it is the optics of it all. Considering the striking similarity between their respective jokes and the showbiz reality that some folks who don't much like O'Brien just might be tempted to believe the worst of him in this situation, O'Brien's side might find the idea of a settlement not to be a bad one after all. A successful show like Conan would likely prefer to avoid the unnecessary distraction and embarrassment of this kind of pesky argument with a guy like Kaseberg.

In the end, it's not that hard to observe that when it comes to protecting jokes in comedy, not much help is available under the copyright law. By comparison to what is done for movies and music, the protection afforded to comedy jokes is rather quite weak. By the way, as matters stand in comedy at this time, if somebody in O'Brien's position (or any other person accused of joke theft) is in the mood to steal jokes and is worried about copyright lawsuits from folks like Kaseberg, all they have to do is to simply use different words to say the same joke and (get this!) they'd be home free. With a copyright scenario like that, it just seems that the notion of protecting jokes in the comedy world at the moment is perhaps nothing less than a big joke in itself.

ACCUSING CONAN O'BRIEN, PART TWO:
When Principle Meets Reality

California
May 17, 2019

We could have seen this coming: Conan O'Brien will eventually blink in his staring contest with Robert Alexander Kaseberg, the man who accused him of stealing jokes from his Twitter and blog platforms and including them in an opening monologue on O'Brien's TBS show. As a matter of fact, in the previous story, I had precisely predicted the current outcome of this case back in November 2015, a few months after the lawsuit was filed.

The predicted outcome is now upon us with the announcement on May 9 that the parties have settled the case that had been set for trial on May 28 in federal court in San Francisco. Among the five stolen jokes cited in Kaseberg's lawsuit was the one about footballer Tom Brady re-gifting his Super Bowl MVP truck to an opposing team coach, plus, one about the shrinking height of the Washington Monument in cold temperatures and one involving a struggle aboard a Delta Airline flight. Kaseberg claimed these jokes were stolen from him between late 2014 and early 2015.

In what seemed like a victory lap, Kaseberg issued a statement saying he was proud that his case helped shed light on an issue facing all comedy writers and that he was happy to be part of contributing legal precedent on the issue of protection afforded to jokes.

For his part, on May 9, O'Brien penned a column on the website *Variety* titled "Why I Decided to Settle a Lawsuit Over Alleged Joke Stealing," in which he explained his decision to walk away from the ring. He essentially said his priority was to "defend the integrity and honesty" of his "remarkably hard working and decent" writers for whom this episode had been "upsetting" in addition to four years and countless legal bills.

Although O'Brien's action was predictable, it seems quite unfortunate that he was forced to call it quits, even though he probably believed that he was more likely than not to eventually win the case on the merits. Before he buckled, he appeared determined to stick up for principles and fight the case on its merits. Sadly, principles appear to have lost its present battle against cold reality.

Anyone who understands the challenge of doing comedy in the internet age of Twitter and other social media would easily appreciate how much O'Brien was in a pickle here. As O'Brien rightly noted in his *Variety* column, comedians who make jokes about the same events can sometimes render these jokes in more or less similar ways or even words. This is the so-called "parallel thought" phenomenon. O'Brien cites an instance from twenty-four years earlier involving himself and David Letterman and Jay Leno all feasting on the same Dan Quayle joke when the former Veep announced he was not running for president. O'Brien even recounted fifteen separate situations discovered by his staffers where Kaseberg himself had tweeted similar jokes to those already rendered on O'Brien's show. (Incidentally, if O'Brien would have chosen to fight on in this case, these incidents might all be part of his defenses and they'd be helpful ones.)

In a copyright lawsuit like O'Brien's case, part of what the plaintiff is required to show is that the alleged joke thief did in fact have access to the material stolen. With an open forum like Twitter to which the entire world potentially has access, it is a cake walk to prove that somebody else had access to an earlier post on Twitter. What an easy advantage for any plaintiff at the starting gate.

And the actual litigation itself would have been a major pain for O'Brien. Both he and his writers probably would have had to testify plus expert testimony and more. Aside from the stress and legal expenses, the sheer drama and uncertainty of testimony and its media coverage are not pretty things. Considering that Kaseberg is a relative unknown who could surely use the limelight afforded by this fight, it becomes obvious that he and of course the high-priced lawyers involved (probably on O'Brien's side) rather than O'Brien himself would be the true beneficiaries from all this. Needless to say, despite his better-than-even odds of winning the lawsuit, O'Brien was looking at what could only be described as a pyrrhic victory.

In the end, O'Brien seemed to have had no choice but to cut his losses. Yet, it bears noting that O'Brien's dilemma here is something of a sad commentary on the state of the law on joke stealing even in our contemporary age of Twitter.

THE DEFEAT OF MATT HOSS: A Copyright Lesson for Comedians

New York
November 6, 2017

Nowadays we live in a new era of comedy where copying a comedian's work can seem like removing money from his pocket. Needless to say, this is the sort of situation where the aggressor can expect some pretty hard pushback. Yet, as comedian Matt Hoss (full name: Matt Hosseinzadeh) learned not that long ago, just because a comedian thinks that somebody else has crossed the line does not make it so—at least as far as the law is concerned.

In May 2016, the edgy comedian Matt Hoss (aka "The Bold Guy" or the "Pick-Up Artist"), filed a copyright violation case in federal court in Manhattan against Ethan and Hila Klein, the producers of the YouTube channel H3H3 Productions. Hoss essentially alleged that the Klein duo by taking way too much of the contents of his earlier video titled *"Bold Guy vs. Parkour Girl"* for inclusion in their latter reaction video (a 13-minute work which sought to satirize his said earlier video), had thereby committed a violation of his copyright in the video. Hoss's lawsuit also tagged on some less significant claims against the Kleins, including defamation.

After the Klein team, a married duo, got word of the lawsuit out to their more than four million subscribers, they responded by floating a GoFundMe campaign that reportedly netted over $160, 000 for the Kleins' legal defense of Hoss's lawsuit. The cause célèbre here? "Fair use" concerns on YouTube.

Explaining his lawsuit, Hoss claimed: "You can essentially watch my film by watching their video. That frustrates the entire point of copyright. Critiquing or commenting on a film should not, and almost always does not, use virtually the entire work." Well, let's just say the court didn't see it that way; otherwise, Hoss would have had a better day in court rather than a big defeat.

Indeed, the decision of the federal court in the case turned out to be a big win for the "fair use" folks and their crowdfunding campaign: In late August, the court ruled that H3H3's actions were protected under the "fair use" doctrine. The judge explained that a review of H3H3's reaction video showed that it amounted to a critical commentary upon the Hoss video, and that it was not a market substitute for the Hoss video, contrary to Hoss' claim that one can watch his film by simply watching the reaction video.

To be sure, the defeat of Hoss' lawsuit isn't at all surprising. In a place like America where the First Amendment is a big deal and offers protections to both comedians and non-comedians alike, a doctrine like "fair use" serves as an important tool for the promotion of free expression and debate in the public square. (Some critics, though, who perceive H3H3 as bullies, have frowned upon the fact that even sometimes spiteful actors like the Kleins are granted free speech protections for their offensive work.) In the copyright context, a person using somebody else's copyrighted work doesn't necessarily need the permission of the owner of the earlier work. Nor does the person have to say something nice about the earlier work. They can be as snarky as they want to be. As a matter of fact, such a person is protected as long as he is merely doing a commentary upon or critique of the said work.

Anyhow, from the court's decision, it is clear that Hoss fell into a common error among copyright plaintiffs regarding the exact extent of the copyright protection that their work enjoys. The problem is made worse by the fact that assessing a doctrine like "fair use" in any litigation is typically a "fact-intensive" inquiry, as the lawyers would say. It is generally a case-by-case situation, meaning that no set-formula exists beforehand for making the call in each case. So, one thing to keep in mind is that just because somebody has copied another person's copyrighted work for inclusion in their own production does not mean that they've run the red light yet. Not even in a situation where the second work has copied a whole lot from the first work, as noted above. As the court made clear, the second work is allowed to use as much of the first work as is necessary to accomplish what the court called the "transformative purpose of critical commentary" on the first work. (As we all know, to *transform* something is "to change or alter" the said thing.)

In practical terms, determining how much is needed for such purpose depends both on the "context" of the work and the "utility" of the portion copied. In plain language, the second person is allowed to copy as much as he needs in order for the portion copied from the first work to make sense in the second work. Incidentally, speaking of "reaction videos" in a battle between YouTube channels, it bears noting that if the second work simply copied and presented the first work to its viewers with very little or no commentary or criticism of the first work, then it's difficult to say that it is a transformation of the first work.

In such situations the second work would be putting itself in a position where it literally becomes a substitute for the first work in the marketplace. In our case here, it would mean that folks looking to watch Hoss's video might as well just watch H3H3's video instead. This sort of situation is a no-no and goes against the very purpose of copyright protection. If that would have happened in this case, it would have resulted in a likely win for Matt Hoss. But the court said it didn't.

As noted above, Hoss also made a few other claims in this case which were decided against him, including the claim of defamation. For instance, the defamation claim was simply tossed out because the statements he alleged as defamatory toward him were ruled as pure statements of opinion rather than facts, which were made by Ethan Klein. Nonetheless, the fact remains that the real meat of Hoss' case here was always the copyright claim.

In the end, the simple lesson here is that copyright protection is not intended to give the owner absolute dominion (or control) over the copyrighted work, meaning that not every case of copying amounts to a copyright violation. As noted above, when the second work can be said to represent a transformation of the first work, there likely is no violation. Translation: someone who is simply lifting somebody else's work without adding anything to it is, well, probably running the red light of copyright law.

SOUTH PARK: Funny Lessons from a Court Face-off

Wisconsin
March 13, 2012

Not long ago, *South Park*, one of Comedy Central's better-liked shows and one that is pretty big on spoofs, got the station and its parent company Viacom in what seemed like a bit of trouble. Some courtroom trouble, that is. And by the time the dust settled on the entire controversy, Viacom found itself not looking so noble thanks to certain positions it had previously taken on exactly what copyright infringement means in the age of You Tube.

Now, some background: In November 2010, music video producer Brownmark Films sued Comedy Central, Viacom and the producers of *South Park*, Matt Stone and Trey Parker, alleging copyright infringement against them and seeking a permanent injunction as well as damages. Brownmark claimed that a 2008 episode of *South Park*, titled Canada on Strike, improperly copied its own music video titled *What (In the Butt)*, a surprisingly popular viral music video that Brownmark made in 2007 that starred the singer Samwell.

Incidentally, both music videos were posted on You Tube, the same company that Viacom had sued for a billion dollars in March 2007 for alleged copyright infringement. Before that lawsuit was dismissed in June 2010, Viacom had raised many eyebrows for claiming that once any video was posted on You Tube, that would automatically make You Tube guilty of copyright infringement even if You Tube didn't know that such a video was violating somebody else's copyright. Wrong! The court ended up telling Viacom that You Tube would only be guilty in such cases if the true copyright owner informs You Tube that the stuff running on its platform was stolen and You Tube still fails to take it down. Well, that was five short months before Brownmark sued Viacom for copyright infringement over the *South Park* episode in question.

140

Aside from the irony of Viacom the hunter now becoming the hunted, this case is a good lesson for folks who might want to know when using stuff found on You Tube could be said to cross the line into copyright infringement. A win for Brownmark here would have created a policing nightmare for You Tube as it would have had to investigate the copyright status of every video submitted to it. As the lawyers would say, You Tube would have become an insurer for every video posted on its platform. Pretty tough stuff! Fortunately for You Tube's lovers and users alike, Brownmark's chances of winning the fight were slim from the start and its end of the road came in July 2011 when the federal court in Wisconsin tossed the lawsuit.

But why did Brownmark lose? Well, quite simply, the court just didn't think there was enough "copying" of one work by the other to amount to the kind of violation that would be punished by the law. And the court went out of its way to really stick it to Brownmark, relying on what's called the "fair use doctrine" under the copyright law. To put it in layman's terms, "fair use" occurs under copyright law when an earlier work is used by a latter work for the purpose of commentary, parody, education, or some other purpose whose main goal is not to secure financial gain for the second work. Of course, when fair use is involved, there's no need to get the copyright owner's permission.

In the *South Park* case, the court said that the episode that Brownmark was complaining about was merely a "parody" of *What (In the Butt)*. In a rather tough and dismissive language, the court said that the whole point of the episode in *South Park* was just "to lampoon the recent craze in our society of watching video clips on the internet that are...to be kind...of rather low artistic sophistication and quality."

When a copyright case is being defended on the basis of "fair use," one of the big factors that are weighed on the scale is the extent or degree of the "copying" involved. Needless to say, the more the second work copies from the first work, the bigger its problems become. This is because the more copying that the second work does from the first work the more it looks like the owners of the second work are, let's say, reaching deeper into the wallet of the owners of the first work and grabbing their money. Here, we are dealing with notions of copying and market share. In the *South Park* case, the court didn't think it was that big of a deal for *South Park* to have copied less than one minute out of Brownmark's twenty-five-minute work.

So, Brownmark lost, and it was a quick defeat. But suppose the copyright claim would have been brought, not by Brownmark but instead by the singer Samwell himself. What then? Well, the court didn't have to decide that question since it looks like the folks behind *South Park* got the proper permission from Samwell to use the song. That saved them the trouble of having to fight on that front. Yet, given the way the court looked at the case both from the perspective of "fair use" under the Copyright Act as well as the First Amendment, which protects "parody," it looks like the result would have been the same, regardless of who's bringing the copyright claim. The court said there was no improper "copying," period!

Still, Viacom and Comedy Central may not be the only winners here. Brownmark also won something which may have been its main purpose all along, given the rather disparaging statement that Brownmark released against Viacom when it launched its lawsuit, plus the fact that their case was weak from the start, something they had to have known. As it happens, the lawsuit gave Brownmark the opportunity to perhaps teach Viacom a lesson by shining a harsh spotlight on Viacom as a company that literally speaks out of both sides of its mouth and tries to have things both ways. As the derisive narrative goes, first, Viacom attacks You Tube for letting folks post stuff on You Tube's platform without clearance from the copyright owners. Then Viacom itself (through its subsidiary Comedy Central) dips into the same You Tube pool and lifts a video from the platform without clearance from Brownmark, the copyright owner. And then, when Viacom is confronted by Brownmark, it takes cover under the notions of "fair use" and "parody." And it wins. How convenient!

In the end, though, there is much more at stake in this case than just whether Viacom is a straight shooter that plays by fair rules. The big thing here really is about allowing folks who are blessed with a creative impulse to utilize stuff publicly available on You Tube and other forums, and not have to worry too much about unnecessary copyright lawsuits. So, despite Viacom's aggressive behaviors in the past, this is one lawsuit that folks who use stuff posted on You Tube or those who simply enjoy checking out stuff posted on You Tube should be genuinely happy for Viacom—an old nemesis in the YouTube posting wars—to win.

THE HANGOVER MOVIE: Reeling from Some Hangovers

California
December 15, 2011

Talk about what's in a name lately, and *The Hangover Part 2* movie easily jumps to mind. The comedy movie has done better-than-expected business at the box office, yet it seems to remain 'hung over' with baggage from its past. Since releasing the movie last May, it has been as if every time the producers turn around, somebody is serving them court papers and demanding something. First, somebody sued them over Ed Harris' face tattoo in the movie. Then another person sued them for injuries he claimed he suffered on the set of the movie. And now, yet another person is suing them, this time claiming that the producers stole the movie's concept or idea from him, and he is looking to yank the movie from the official records.

In the latest lawsuit filed last October, an aspiring filmmaker named Michael Alan Rubin is suing the makers of the movie [the Warner Bros. studio; the director and the writers] in federal court in California for copyright infringement and for defamation. Rubin, who is also suing his estranged wife, claims that that the makers of the movie stole the idea of the movie from his own movie treatment Mickey and Kirin, which was based on his own life experiences. For his troubles, Rubin is taking no prisoners: he wants the certificate of copyright registration for the movie to be yanked plus damages and a court order banning any further sale or distribution of the movie.

Now, some background: In real life, Rubin claims that, in 2007, he had gone to Japan to marry his Asian girlfriend in a traditional ceremony and then traveled with her on a honeymoon to Thailand and India. The couple then broke up on their honeymoon and Rubin ended up on the Indian vacation haven of Goa where he picked up acting gigs and worked on a movie treatment that detailed his life experiences with his wife.

So, that's his case. For the moment Rubin's lawsuit is not looking like such a heavy duty, high voltage case. Yet a win for him could mean that it gets pretty dicey going forward for any filmmakers to make movies based on events in somebody's life even if the movies are billed as fiction. But he has to win first. And what are the odds that Rubin will in fact win? Well, not so great, it seems.

For starters, the defamation branch of his case looks weaker than the copyright side, which isn't exactly a good horse to bet on either. Rubin's defamation claim seems a bold one: He claims that *The Hangover Part 2* movie damaged his reputation by portraying him as a guy who would do drugs and have sex with a transsexual prostitute. To win his defamation claim, Rubin needs to show that the movie made a false statement of fact that damaged his reputation in the community. But his first real hurdle with this claim will be the effort to prove that he was indeed the person being portrayed in the movie. If he can't hack it, then that's the end of the road for his claim. And since the movie is billed as fiction and Rubin wasn't mentioned by name or identified in any other way in the movie, he faces an uphill battle getting this job done. Things might have been easier for Rubin with his defamation claim against a Hollywood movie if both he and the story of his misadventures in Asia would have been well known to the public.

Then there's the copyright side of his case. Quite simply, in order to win a copyright infringement case, the person filing the lawsuit has to show that the other person copied an original work that belonged to him. In these situations, the courts look at the two works to see just how similar they are. And it is not enough to show that the second work has something in common with the first one. The person filing the lawsuit will lose if he cannot show that the similarities between the two works are more than just minor stuff. He'll be sitting very pretty with his case if he can show that the similarities are rather striking in nature in such a way that it will be tough to chalk it all up to mere coincidence. Plus, he also has to show that the person he is suing had actual access to the first work, which would have given that person the opportunity to copy the work.

The sort of situation that would easily come to mind here is the old Letty Lynton case from the 1930s (which starred Joan Crawford) where a movie that was supposed to be based on a book ended up having more in common with a play of the same name than with the book itself. For instance, while the lead character in the said book poisoned her male lover with arsenic, the same lead character in both the play and the movie itself (get this!) poisoned her male lover with a different substance, which however wasn't arsenic. Add to this the fact that the book, the play, and the movie were all set in the same society and at the same period in time. With respect to access, it also happened that the filmmakers bought their right to base their movie on the book only after attempting but failing to buy the right to base the movie on the play.

In Rubin's case, his life experiences obviously remain fair game for movie makers and book writers. But, of course, it's a different story if he can manage to reduce his life experiences into something that can be protected by copyright, for instance, by putting it down in writing or in some other fixed form. So, is his so-called movie treatment Mickey and Kirin in a form where it can be protected by copyright? Maybe so! (Rubin claims he registered the thing with the Writers Guild of America.) And if so, did the filmmakers have access to the material? Here, Rubin claims that his ex-wife had ties to the filmmakers and would have been their source for the material. Can he prove that? By the way, assuming Rubin's ex-wife simply told his life story to the filmmakers who then made it into a film, it seems like that wouldn't be a copyright infringement issue.

If Rubin passes these gateway tests by answering these questions, then the court will get into the big question of the day, which is whether the second work (the *Hangover* movie) was copied from the earlier work (Rubin's Mickey and Kirin movie treatment). Is there a 'striking' similarity between the two? As already noted, minor stuff or matters of mere coincidence just won't cut it. All these questions make for a tough road ahead for Rubin's copyright claim. Funny thing is, the gateway questions may well be harder to crack than the big question itself.

In the end, it is clear that none of this stuff will be a cake walk for Rubin. And his odds of winning are rather long. Luckily for the movie, this latest claim against the movie also seems to be weakest link in the chain of attacks so far against the movie. Yet, for all its box office success, it is interesting to see just how many "hangovers" are trailing the movie. At the rate things are going, who knows what next lawsuit just might be lurking around the corner for *The Hangover Part 2*. Talk about something living up to its name.

CASE UPDATE: On December 19, 2011, the *Hollywood Reporter*, quoting court records, reported that the plaintiff, Michael Alan Rubin, had voluntarily dismissed his lawsuit against Warner Bros. However, there was no indication in the report as to whether the dismissal of the case was preceded by an out-of-court settlement of the matter.

COMEDIANS GETTING IN TROUBLE ONSTAGE AND OFFSTAGE

CHAPTER FOUR

COMEDIANS GETTING IN TROUBLE ONSTAGE AND OFFSTAGE

Again, as we saw earlier, comedians enjoy a lot of legal protection for the things they say onstage and [sometimes] offstage, even if those things cause a lot of irritation to people who may feel wounded by them. And despite their battles with the so-called political correctness (PC) brigade, comedians still recognize and treasure just how much they are allowed to say under the law. However, *saying* whatever one feels like saying and *doing* whatever one feels like doing are two different things with different consequences. So then, what does the law do when a comedian "gets a wild hair" either onstage or off stage and actually does something physical, and wrong, to other people?

The cases in this section show how the law handles those situations in which comedians cross over from the safe zone where they can say offensive things to people to the tricky zone where they actually do offensive physical things to other people. To be sure, crossing this kind of line is usually a teachable moment for most comedians. From Andy Dick wearing a skirt and shoving some guy's head into his exposed crotch to Katt Williams storming off a show stage, ripping off his shirt and challenging audience members to a fight, the all-too recurring lesson is that in those situations, comedians, unfortunately, forfeit the prized protection that they would normally enjoy under the First Amendment for the things they simply say. Instead, they are held to the same standard of liability as everybody else when they do act out.

* * *

ANDY DICK, THE DEFENDANT: When a Comedian Goes Off the Deep End

Texas
July 7, 2011

Comedian Andy Dick is in trouble again. Only this time, he is not being arrested by the cops, but is being sued by someone who won't take his antics lying down.

In early May, a Dallas man named Robert Tucker filed a lawsuit against Dick, his agent the United Talent Agency (UTA), and a Dallas club named Trees where Dick had a show this past December. In the lawsuit, Tucker seeks damages against Dick, UTA and Trees for offensive physical contact, intentional infliction of emotional distress and defamation by conduct, plus separate claims for negligence against UTA and Trees, and yet another claim in premises liability against Trees.

In December 2010, Dick was performing at a nightclub in Dallas, Texas, and was dressed in a red skirt (wearing no underwear) plus a black top and a wig. Then, as Dick moved among the audience, Tucker asked him for an autograph. Dick then allegedly pulled up a bar stool beside Tucker and proceeded to force his genitals against the left side of Tucker's face. The night before, Dick reportedly pulled the same act in another club in Austin, Texas, when, while standing onstage, he pulled another patron's head into his groin.

The claim against Dick in his personal capacity gives Tucker his best chance of winning something in this lawsuit. Under the law, an offensive physical contact or battery occurs when one person deliberately makes physical contact with another person without their consent and without lawful excuse. Also, an intentional infliction of emotional distress situation occurs where one person does a wrongful act so egregious and "outrageous" that it crosses the line of decency and what can be "tolerated in a civilized society."

Defamation by conduct occurs where one person's conduct damages the other person's reputation by creating the false impression that the other person either is or did something they did not in fact do. At the minimum it seems that Dick may well be liable for causing an offensive physical contact or battery, as he obviously didn't have Tucker's consent to do what he did to him, and it is hard to see what lawful excuse he might have had for his actions. And Dick's odds of beating the other claims against him are not so good.

But the case against UTA (his agent) and Trees (the club that booked him) is not so straightforward and is a harder case to win. Here, the plaintiff seems to be trying to make the folks who do business with Dick accountable for his "bad boy" behavior by roping them in along with Dick under a theory called "vicarious liability," which holds people liable for the actions of others. And Tucker is making a big deal of the fact both UTA and Trees knew of Dick's bad boy behavior and that they still arranged shows for him just so they can make money off his bad behavior.

But the catch here is that "vicarious liability" claims usually cover master-servant relationships, as in employer or employee situations where the employee is subject to the "control" and direction of the employer. In this case, Dick as a comedian is more of an "independent contractor" merely doing business with UTA and Trees, and so is not their employee.

Plus, when we are dealing with an intentional (mis)conduct, like the actions taken by Dick in this case, it is hard to show that one person authorized another to commit a wrongful act (or "tort"), especially when the person who committed the wrongful act is not an employee but an independent contractor. Again, since Dick is not an employee of either UTA or Trees, and he is not subject to their control and direction in the way he did his job as a comedian. So Tucker's claim against them for negligence in choosing to work with Dick despite their knowing about his past behavior likely won't get far.

But of all the claims against Dick's business partners here, the case against Trees for premises liability is the one that in other circumstances just might have some legs. This is because having paid money to watch the show, Tucker is an "invitee" to the club and Trees, as an occupier of land, owes him a duty to take steps to keep the premises safe for his visit. Yet, that duty does not cover all circumstances and would only extend to dangers that the club owner could prevent. This is because Trees the club is not an insurer for Tucker or anyone's safety, so to speak.

And regardless of what Trees may have known about Dick's past behavior, it is hard to demonstrate that Trees could have foreseen and prevented Dick's sudden and unexpected mistreatment of a member of the audience who had merely asked for his autograph. To try to make such a case would seem like a stretch: After all, it's not as if we are talking here about, say, a loose overhead electric bulb falling onto Tucker's head while he was sitting inside the club. Quite simply, Dick, and Dick alone, is the problem here. Period!

In the end, the obvious lesson for comedians from this case is that as far as consequences go, there is a line between what they say and what they do—whether onstage or offstage. Translation: though they may not get in trouble for making offensive and outrageous remarks while doing a shtick onstage (thanks to the First Amendment), comedians—just like everybody else—may yet get in trouble for acting out in physical ways.

CASE UPDATE: On March 26, 2013, Andy Dick's side reached a settlement with Robert Tucker, and the court agreed to dismiss the case with prejudice, meaning it cannot be filed again. The terms of the settlement were confidential.

GEORGE WALLACE'S LAWSUIT: A Million-Dollar Lesson at the Bellagio

Nevada
July 27, 2014

This past April, something really nice happened to George Wallace: A friendly nod from a Las Vegas jury made the funnyman more than a million dollars richer and sent him smiling to his bank. And for working comics everywhere who either travel for gigs around the country or do their gigs locally, Wallace's win is certainly good news not least because it could happen to them in a similar situation. But the case also offers an opportunity for most industry observers to consider the other kinds of circumstances that could arise when working comics are hired to perform gigs at any venue. As it happens, each of these circumstances carries different consequences for the comedians as well as the venues that hire them. But first, here's the story:

In December 2007, Wallace, the longtime resident showman at The Flamingo in Las Vegas, was hired to perform at a private party at a casino resort, the Bellagio, also in Las Vegas. However, sometime during the performance, Wallace tripped on some loose wires onstage and ruptured his Achilles tendon. Following his injuries, Wallace sued the Bellagio for negligence, claiming damages for loss of earnings in the present and in the future, medical expenses as well as for pain and suffering. This past April, after a full trial, the jury found the Bellagio liable for negligence and awarded Wallace the sum of $1.3 million. To be sure, Wallace's injuries from his fall were not a joke at all: aside from enduring tremendous pain and suffering, Wallace was also forced to quit doing his long running show at the Flamingo.

Before considering other situations that comedians might encounter when they go out to do gigs, perhaps it is useful to start by looking at why Wallace won his court case in the first place.

For starters, when a person files an action for negligence, like Wallace did against the Bellagio, his point (in plain terms) is that the other person he is suing has failed to exercise the level of care that the law requires people in those kinds of situations to exercise for the benefit and protection of other people. In each negligence lawsuit, the person who is suing is often the person who has been injured due to the carelessness of the person being sued. Needless to say, in order for the person who is alleged to have been negligent (or "careless" as a lay person would say) to be on the hook for damages, the other person must have sustained an actual injury. No injury, no damages.

In Wallace's case, the negligence (or want of due care) that he alleges against the Bellagio was that loose wires were allowed to be present onstage, which then caused him to stumble during his performance. Speaking of the level of care required in these kinds of situations, the law applies the standard of a "reasonable person" in each situation. In this case, the jury's verdict in favor of Wallace means the jury thought that a reasonable venue in Bellagio's position would not allow loose cables onstage during a comedian's performance any more than a reasonable store in Walmart's position or Duane Reade's position would allow puddles of water on the floor of their aisle during business hours when customers are present. In nailing the Bellagio for negligence, Wallace had the good fortune that some employee of the Bellagio itself had taken photos of the stage after the performance, which showed loose cables coming out of two speakers. "Thank God for that employee at the Bellagio," Wallace remarked.

And when injury occurs in a negligence claim, a plaintiff like Wallace could actually claim damages for lost income both backwards and forwards against a defendant like the Bellagio. (Plus, of course, damages for things like pain and suffering and medical expenses.) In Wallace's case, he sought millions of dollars in damages, first for the earnings he lost because of his injury and then for all the money he won't be making in the future because of his injury.

Well, he ended up not getting as much money as he'd originally asked because, obviously, it all comes down to what the jury believes is fair. In this case, the jury gave Wallace $1.3 million for lost income, pain and suffering and his medical bills. Interestingly, the jury gave nothing to Wallace for his expected loss of earnings in the future. Why? The simple answer: "He was back to making the money he was making before," explained the jury foreman. (Wallace's view that the injury had caused him to walk with a permanent limp apparently did not sway the jury when it came to matters like his claim for future earnings.)

As indicated above, aside from what happened to Wallace, there are other situations where comedians who are out there performing gigs could face some trouble onstage. Now, what if, for instance, somebody in the audience at the Bellagio would have attacked Wallace and beaten him up while he was onstage because of something he said. Suppose that Wallace was so badly injured during such an attack that he couldn't perform his gigs for a while. Could he, in those circumstances, have been able to go after the Bellagio seeking damages for his injuries? Well, as tempting as it might be to say he could sue them, the correct answer is most likely that he can't. For starters, he wouldn't be able to sue the Bellagio for negligence because here we're not talking about some accident or some other case where the Bellagio failed to exercise reasonable care for his protection. Rather, we are dealing with what would be an "intentional act" by somebody else for whom the hotel would not be responsible. The attack here would be an assault and battery, which is an intentional tort. Generally, event venues like the Bellagio and others are not held liable for those kinds of random acts perpetrated by patrons at their facility. Why? Because they usually would not have foreseen such outbursts in advance and therefore couldn't have been able to prevent them.

Yet it doesn't mean that the attacker would go scot-free. In such a case, Wallace would simply have to sue him directly for damages for assault and battery and take his chances that the guy isn't some loser who has no ability to pay any jury award that Wallace might win against him. (Of course, it would be a different case if, for instance, Wallace would have been beaten up and robbed by muggers on Bellagio's premises. In that case, Bellagio will be liable, because we'd be back talking about negligence and the liability of owners of premises in situations where their premises are allowed to be unsafe for visitors. And we'd be dealing with matters happening offstage rather than onstage.)

However, it is worth noting that there can also be a flip side to these encounters, especially since we're talking about showbiz situations where matters can sometimes escalate rather quickly. In some situations, it may be that the comedian himself is the aggressor, perhaps against somebody in the audience. (One may recall how the comedy legend Richard Pryor reportedly once jumped off the stage during a performance and stabbed a guy in the audience with a fork. Why? The hapless guy had allegedly heckled Mr. Pryor. Then in a different instance, another comic Andy Dick stepped off the stage during a performance and decided to mingle with the audience, and while there he grabbed a guy's head and brushed the poor guy's face against his exposed crotch. Well, this time, a lawsuit followed.)

So, when a comedian at a performance does something wrong to a member of the audience, just who gets sued and for what exactly? If you guessed that the offending comedian himself would get sued for assault and battery, you guessed right. No doubt, this one is an easy shot and pretty much anyone can figure that out. But could any of those audience members also turn around and sue the comedy club (or venue) that hired the comedian? Could they, for instance, say that the venue owed them a "duty" to prevent what the comedian did to them? The short answer here is that this one most likely won't wash. Tough luck! Again, as stated above and at the risk of sounding repetitive, a venue will generally not be held liable or responsible for the intentional (and wrongful) act of somebody else. That's because usually situations where somebody just freaks out and does something crazy are generally not foreseeable in advance by those who run the venues. The simple logic here is that if you can't foresee them, then you likely can't prevent them.

Besides, somebody who's been hired to perform as a comedian is more like an "independent contractor" who works for himself and determines how he does his job. He is not like an "employee" of the venue whose wrongful acts or misconduct can be attributed to the venue. Even if the comedian has a special arrangement with the venue to do repeat gigs there, such as the residency deal that Wallace had at the Flamingo, that still does not make him an employee of the venue and he remains an independent contractor who must answer for his own misconduct.

In the end, it is obvious that Wallace's case ended well for him—in a quite enviable million-dollar way. And of course, any other comedian in that situation would have hoped for the same result. Even more than that, in each situation where comedians are out doing gigs, this case seems like a "teachable moment" for both performers and venue owners alike.

KATT WILLIAMS: When a Comedian's Time Onstage May Be Too Small

California
December 14, 2012

Katt Williams is a comedian who is no stranger to run-ins with the law and with other folks. And lately, his run of legal troubles has been adding up: he attacked an aspiring rapper on his tour bus at an Oakland hotel and then (two days later) led cops on a high-speed chase for reckless driving in Sacramento, California. He also got sued by his female personal assistant for allegedly punching her at his house and causing her serious and permanent injuries. But for many comedy watchers, there is one incident in Williams' line-up of recent troubles that raises a new kind of question in the way that comedians relate to their fans. And the answer to that question may be something that comics might want to pay attention to. Here's what happened:

This past November, Williams and events promoter Live Nation collaborated on a comedy gig at the Oracle Arena in Oakland, California, featuring Williams. However, a mere ten minutes into his set, Williams became provoked by the actions of a heckler and reportedly had a serious meltdown. As the story went, he took off his clothes and challenged the audience itself to a fight, and then attempted to fight at least three members of the audience. Needless to say, by the time the fracas ended, the show itself was over as well. The fans were not the least bit amused. In response, a disappointed audience member named Brian Herline, acting on behalf of all the other audience members who attended the flopped event, filed a lawsuit against both Williams and Live Nation.

For starters, the class action nature of this lawsuit is something that should be pretty easy to maintain and Herline and his posse likely won't have a problem with it. The device of a class action is meant to allow folks who have suffered a "common injury or

161

loss from a common source" to pull their resources together in order to obtain whatever relief or remedy they are entitled to get under the law. So, in this case, as long as the audience members (the plaintiffs) keep themselves on the same page, they'll be just fine. But, of course, if, for instance, some of them are seeking a refund of their ticket price while others are claiming damages for assault and battery, then the lawsuit can no longer survive as a class action. The simple explanation for that would be that if the people bringing the lawsuit together are actually seeking different kinds of remedies from the court, it implies that they probably suffered different kinds of losses as well.

Anyhow, what we have in this case seems like a proper class action in which all the audience members are reportedly seeking unspecified damages for "Katt Williams' non-performance." To put it in laypersons' terms, Williams and Live Nation are being sued for not living up to their promise to Herline and the other audience members who attended the event to see a show. But what exactly did the comedian and his promoters promise to the audience? Well, first of all, when people talk about *promise* in this way, it implies that there is some sort of agreement between the two sides: the comedian and his promoters on the one part and the audience members on the other part.

In this context, it is fair to say that paying money to see a comedian's performance may be no different from paying money to see a movie. In the movie case, we can assume that in exchange for the moviegoer's ticket price, he is promised a chance to see the movie he has paid for. Since the moviegoer's deal is simply to see the movie, if he happens not to like the movie after he sees it, then tough luck. Of course, if the movie theater does not keep its promise to show him a movie or doesn't show him the whole movie, then the moviegoer is entitled to "rescind" or cancel the contract and receive "damages" in return. Typically, the damages he would receive in this situation is the chance to get his ticket price back. Translation: there are two promises in this situation and each promise is the price or consideration for the other promise. Simple as that!

Similarly, in the situation involving a comedian and a paying audience, the understanding is that in exchange for the cover charge that the audience pays, they get a chance to see the comedian perform. Clearly, what a comedian's audience is promised is a chance to see the comedian perform. And just as in the case with the movie, whether or not the comedian's audience like the performance they get is a different matter altogether. But again, just like the movie theater, the comedian and his promoters must at least deliver a performance. This is where Williams and Live Nation may have a real problem in this case.

The big question here is: Did they at least deliver a performance that day considering that Williams went bonkers after just ten minutes, got mixed up in a fracas and brought the show to an end? Could it be a defense in Williams' favor that a heckler interfered with the show? Well, the odds are not looking too good for Williams' side with these questions.

Usually, when a comedian is sued for damages for non-performance in a case like this one, it is essentially a breach of contract action. And in a breach of contract case, the person sued might choose to play the hand that his efforts to deliver the thing he had promised was frustrated by the actions of the person to whom the promise was made. In this case, a guy in Williams' position might try to say that his attempt to give his performance was frustrated by hecklers who were members of the audience. But will that be a good enough defense? Probably not! Because when the court begins to look at the whole case, part of what it could consider is something called "custom or usage" in the industry—namely, what the usual practice is among comedians at a performance.

As it happens, hecklers are known to be a problem at comedy performances. Yet, as a practical matter, hecklers can always be removed from the venue of a performance, in much the same way as somebody who's trying to disrupt a theater performance on Broadway or someone heckling an invited speaker at a college campus. Besides, a "reasonable" professional comedian would be expected to find a less disruptive way to handle a heckler rather than to take the heckler's bait, walk off the stage and challenge the audience to fights. In short, considering that Williams' actions do not seem reasonable under the circumstances, especially when judged by the standards of other professional comics in similar situations, the defense of blame-the-heckler likely won't be available to him.

Still, there may be more to this case by the time the dust settles down: Williams' problem may not end with just giving back the audience's ticket prices to them. Aside from that contract law situation, Williams just may have committed a tort as well (A *tort* is simply some wrongful act that breaches a duty owed to somebody else.) For instance, any instance of actual fighting with any members of the audience would likely have rendered him liable for the tort of "assault and battery."

By definition, an assault occurs whenever one person puts another person in fear of imminent physical contact. On the other hand, a battery occurs where one person actually makes an offensive physical contact with another person without the consent of that other person, or without any lawful justification for making that kind of contact. There seems to be little doubt that none of the audience members at the event consented to Williams' actions toward them. Plus, it is hard to see what lawful justification (such as, maybe, self-defense or something else) that Williams could have had for his aggressive actions toward the audience. So, if Williams did stop at merely challenging specific folks in the audience to fights, as the lawsuit seems to suggest, then he is perhaps liable only for an assault. In that kind of situation, since he didn't actually make physical contact with anyone, he'll be spared the more serious hassle of an actual battery claim.

As long as we are talking about claims against Live Nation for Williams' actions, the assault and battery claims will not lie against them. Otherwise, to say that Live Nation will be liable for these actions will mean creating "vicarious liability" against them for the actions of Williams. Vicarious liability is normally reserved for situations where one person controls and directs the actions of another person such as the sorts of situations that exists between a master and a servant or between an employer and an employee.

In the case we have here, it is clear that even though Live Nation brought Williams to the show, Williams was not an employee or servant of Live Nation. This means that he was not subject to their control and direction in the way he did his job. So, as a professional comedian, Williams remained an independent contractor throughout the event. Actions like going offstage and threatening to fight folks in the audience is an "intentional" act and the law will not hold promoters like Live Nation liable for the intentional wrongdoing of an independent contractor.

This case is also sort of unique for another reason. For example, this is a case where a comedian is being sued for what the comedian does at a performance rather than what he says onstage. Obviously, saying and doing stuff are two different things: What a comic "says" onstage enjoys free speech protection. However, what an irate comic decides to "do" at a performance, whether onstage or offstage, is a different matter altogether. And this is one big reason why Williams is in such a weak position in this case: when he went offstage in a fighting mood, he lost all the normal protections that a comedian would normally enjoy for what he says while onstage. His free speech protections deserted him.

Needless to say, whatever the temptation, it is never a good idea for any comedian to get offstage and confront an audience. One of the biggest things the comedian would lose in such a situation is the protection of First Amendment. As matters stand here, Williams' position in this lawsuit isn't a pretty one. His best move ought to be to find a way to settle this one and just move on.

MIKE EPPS: Onstage with a Process Server

Texas
August 6, 2011

Comedians have a reputation for being weird, and Mike Epps, known for his roles in *The Hangover* and *Jumping the Broom* movies, is no stranger to weird moments. But what happened to him on May 6 was so weird that it caught him totally unawares, perhaps more so because he was performing onstage at the time, and it wasn't just some comedian trouble with some heckler. It was, actually, an officer of the law.

Here's what happened: Epps was in the middle of his shtick that evening at the Verizon Theatre in Grand Prairie, Texas, when a process server walked up to him onstage and served him some court papers, which had summoned him to appear as a defendant in a lawsuit. The process server then walked off but not before Epps gave her a piece of his mind. In an angry outburst caught on a TMZ tape, Epps berated her with choice words like "white b----"and "f--- you" and "suck my d---". (Expletive, expletive, expletive.)

It turns out that back in November 2010, Epps had allegedly gotten into a fight with a photographer in a night club in Detroit, Michigan, and not wanting to let things slide, the photographer had filed a million-dollar lawsuit against him.

Some rather surprised comedians have asked whether it's even legal for process servers to approach comedians onstage and serve them with court papers. Short answer: if the process server can actually get to the comedian onstage and tell him what the papers are about, then, you bet, it is legal. And while it may be an unusual experience for comedians at work onstage, it's not that unusual for other people to get served at work. It actually happens that a guy who works at a post office, a restaurant or at city hall could be served court papers at his job with all the embarrassment that could follow.

What we are talking about here is "due process," and it's a big matter under the constitution. To make it as simple as possible, one can say that under the law, a person who is sued is entitled to be notified of the lawsuit against him so he can get a fair and adequate opportunity to answer the claim. If that is not done, then it means the court has no "personal" jurisdiction over him and any judgment rendered against him will be a waste of time. Any person being sued can be notified of the lawsuit against him in any number of ways, as long as the method that is chosen actually does gives him "notice" of the claim against him. Thus, a person being sued can be served with the court papers wherever he can be found, even outside the state. That means that he does not have to be served at his home and that he could be served at his job. Translation: a comedian, yes, can also be served at his job— onstage, that is.

So, getting access to the person to be sued is the key thing. However, trying to reach performers like comedians onstage is sort of like trying to reach a celebrity rock star at a huge concert, which means having to cut through his bodyguards to serve him with court papers. It's never an easy thing but once the process server or some other authorized person can actually get access to the person to be served, that should do it. Perhaps, in Epps's case, the comedy club owners might have tried stopping the process server from reaching the comedian onstage – if they would have known why she was there in the first place. But, alas, she was able to literally slip through the fence and serve the comedian, and that was that. Done!

How about his remaining options? Well, since he has been served, the court now has "jurisdiction" over him. But Epps can of course try to "set aside" or "quash" the court process on a whole bunch of grounds. For instance, he can try to show that the court papers were perhaps served rather too late on him; or that the court has no power over someone like him, perhaps because he lives outside the court's territory (commonly called "jurisdiction," in legal parlance) and didn't do anything inside the court's said territory; or even that the court has no power to deal with the kind of claim that the photographer is making against him. Yep, lawyers can come up with so many things to oppose the service.

If he is not able to set aside the court papers, then Epps will have to answer the photog's allegations against him. Since they were allegedly in a fight, the photographer's most obvious claim against Epps will be for the tort of battery, which occurs when one person deliberately makes physical contact with another person without their consent and without lawful excuse. Since Epps obviously wouldn't have had the photog's consent to make contact with him, he would have to explain what lawful excuse he had for making physical contact with the guy. If he was acting in self-defense at the time of the fight, or if he hit the photog by accident, that might do the trick. The only problem with offering that line of defense here is that Epps already gloated onstage right after the process server gave him the court papers that "[t]his is from when I whooped that n------'s ass in Detroit." Well, this sort of talk openly admitting to wrongdoing certainly won't help his case one bit.

In the end, one may quarrel with the idea of a comedian being served with court papers onstage, considering all the distractions and pretty unsettling mind games that could come with things like that. Still, while it may be unusual and perhaps unfair to serve comedians with court papers in that situation, it is nonetheless legal, as indicated above. Of course, the photog and the process server in Epp's case were obviously pretty aggressive in the way they moved to haul Epps into court. But then again, lawsuits are not exactly friendly affairs.

WHEN THE FUNNY GOES SILLY

CHAPTER FIVE

WHEN THE FUNNY GOES SILLY

Comedy is a major force in our pop culture today, and its influence shows no sign of slowing down anytime soon. From politically slanted talk shows like *The Daily Show, Gutfeld!,* and *Last Week Tonight with John Oliver* to more traditional late-night shows like Jimmy Fallon's *The Tonight Show Starring Jimmy Fallon* and sketch-heavy shows like the famed *Saturday Night Live,* comedy now seems to increasingly frame our social conversation to the point that sometimes one gets the feeling that the things we talk about are usually just the things that comedians want us to talk about. So, the comedy and pop culture space today have gotten very busy.

Naturally, this tends to create something of a free-for-all atmosphere where both comedians and non-comedians alike appear to be pushing and shoving one another with all kinds of motivations, including publicity, entertainment, money, and whatever. Some of this stuff might well have seemed rather silly and ludicrous to maybe someone from an earlier age in comedy, or even someone from the present age who is, well, sane and normal. But this is where we are with these things in contemporary times and sometimes some of the craziness spills into the courtroom, like when Donald Trump sued Bill Maher to collect on a supposed $5 million bet involving orange orangutan hair.

171

So, we're dealing in this section with stuff that belong in this crazy funny territory, perhaps just the sort of things that sometimes make people wonder if our society is suffering from having too many lawyers. At any rate, here are the cases:

* * *

DONALD TRUMP vs. BILL MAHER: Tensions Between a Joke and a Deal

California
March 10, 2013

When it comes to money matters, mixing things up with Donald Trump can be a costly proposition. This means that even making a bet with the real estate mogul and *Celebrity Apprentice* host can earn someone a court date and maybe even set the person back a couple million dollars. Not even if the bet was meant as a joke. And not even if the person on the opposite side is a well-known comedian. Like Bill Maher.

This past January, Maher, the host of HBO's *Real Time with Bill Maher* appeared on Jay Leno's *The Tonight Show* and mocked Trump as "the spawn of his mother having sex with an orangutan." Maher then said that if Trump could show proof that what he [Maher] said wasn't true, he would give $5 million to Trump, which money the billionaire would be free to donate to any charity of his choice, such as "Hair Club for Men, the Institute for Incorrigible Douchebaggery, whatever charity…" To drive his point home, Maher also claimed that the color of Trump's hair and the color of an orange orangutan were the only two things in nature of the same color. The audience laughed loudly and applauded. And most people regarded Maher's offer as merely mimicking or mocking Trump's own offer a year earlier to donate $5 million to any charity of Barack Obama's choosing if Obama would produce his birth certificate and college transcripts.

Well, as it turned out, if the comedian was joking, the billionaire apparently didn't take it like a joke: Two days later, Trump produced his birth certificate to Maher and then demanded that the funnyman pony up, as promised. When that didn't happen, Trump made a most unexpected move: He sued Maher in a Los Angeles court, for breach of contract.

Lately, it seems like The Donald has been busy trying to teach folks out there some lessons in the courtroom. Last December, just one month before the start of his dust-up with Maher, Trump was awarded $5 million dollars in his lawsuit against ex-beauty queen Sheena Monnin, a former Miss USA contestant, who in June last year pulled out of the pageant after alleging that the competition was fixed. In response, the Trump Organization, owner of the pageant, hit her with a defamation lawsuit, claiming that her false statements had hurt the reputation of the Miss USA Competition. The arbitrator agreed, and ordered Monnin, a former Miss Pennsylvania, to pay $5 million to the Trump Organization.

However, in the comedy industry, Trump's lawsuit against Maher has not won him a lot of admirers. At stake here is the longstanding freedom of comedians to go on comedy talk shows and just parody public figures without even thinking about it. Needless to say, whatever Trump's chances of winning the case, his critics fear that if he wins the lawsuit against Maher, it could open an entirely new door against comedians—a door people had assumed did not even exist. To be sure, this sort of apprehension flows in the same stream as the so-called 'chill' factor on free speech rights in general.

But what are Trump's odds of actually winning? Can he even sue Maher for breach of contract in a situation like this one? For starters, when most folks think about breach of contract, they often imagine a situation where two people have made promises to one another and then one of them either refuses or fails to keep his word. In such situations, the agreement is made ahead of time, with each party knowing exactly what he promises to do and what he gets in return from the other side. Needless to say, they both recognize that the agreement is 'binding' on them and that they can be sued in court if they don't keep their promises. This kind of contract is called a 'bilateral' contract and is obviously not the sort of situation that Trump and Maher are involved in.

But that's not all. There are other situations that might involve people who have never negotiated or 'bargained' with each other, or perhaps have never even known each other or met each other before. Yet, as long as an offer is made by one person and accepted by the other, a contract situation can arise between them. Again, it must be clear to both parties that the agreement is 'binding' on them and that they can be sued in court for not honoring the agreement. Here's a situation where that could happen: Jose loses his dog and offers to pay $200 to anyone who finds and returns his lost dog to him. Three days go by, and Jimmy finds the dog and returns it to Jose. At that point, Jimmy has 'accepted' the contract by actually performing it and Jimmy can sue Jose for breach of contract if he fails to pay up. This kind of contract is called a 'unilateral' contract and it is obviously less commonplace than the other kind of contract, discussed above. And for whatever it is worth, this is the kind of contract that Trump's lawsuit supposes exists between the billionaire and the comedian.

Still, Trump has a real problem here as far as trying to establish that he and Maher entered into a contract. The crucial piece that is missing in their situation is something called "intent to enter into legal relations." Translation: Did Maher intend to make an offer that is 'binding' at law? Usually, when it comes to whether a person means for what he says to stand as a valid offer or promise, the 'context' of the statement can be pretty crucial. Naturally, not every offer will qualify as valid. Consider the case of a "puff" in a product ad. As the court recognized in an old English case from 1893, it is possible that what might seem to one party like a promise or an offer from the other party may well be "only a puff from which no promise to pay could be implied." In a layperson's language, a *puff* is just an exaggeration or swagger about something, and when it comes to offers, stuff like "puffs" are out.

Now, speaking of context and intent, here's the big question in this lawsuit: What is the intent of a comedian making a funny statement on a late-night show in America? Is he looking to make an agreement that is binding upon him at law, even if he's mentioning somebody else by name? The short answer here is that any average person (think "reasonable" person) who understands the nature of American talk shows as well as how comedians generally behave, probably would think the answer is no. More likely, he or she will think that the comedian was merely joking around.

There's another angle to Trump's lawsuit: As he took Maher to court, Trump rejected the idea that Maher may simply have been joking when he made the offer. "I don't think he was joking. He said it with venom." Without directly saying so, this talk about venom seems to hint at malice on the part of Maher. An accusation that somebody made a statement or did something with malice likely would be more relevant and even helpful in a different lawsuit than a breach of contact claim. Because of this, one just might wonder why Trump did not choose to sue Maher for something like defamation instead of breach of contract. By the way, Trump presented his birth certificate in an attempt to show that Maher's statement was false. And we note that a false statement that hurts someone's reputation is the whole point of a defamation claim. Plus, as a billionaire with huge financial interests in the business arena, the money he can recover against someone who has damaged his reputation might be a lot more than $5million. After all, defaming a billionaire like Trump is not like defaming a cabbie or a janitor.

So, why didn't he sue for defamation instead? Well, apparently because Trump is smart—or at least his lawyers are. To be sure, whatever his odds of winning his present breach of contract claim against Maher, his odds of winning a defamation claim against the comedian are even longer. Much longer indeed! A defamation action against a comedian for what he said on another comedian's talk show will quickly be consumed by much legal wrangling and bombast over the First Amendment and free speech. In short, between the notion that Trump is a "public figure," and the other factors that the free speech law concerns itself with, such a messy fight, will most likely end up as a losing proposition for him.

In a defamation kind of situation, either Maher's statement will be found to be a mere joke or parody, given the context in which it was made, or it would be considered as a mere statement of opinion rather than fact. One way or the other the result will be the same for Trump—a defeat! Yet, for all the talk about context, the law, as they often say, remains "an ass," and one can imagine a situation where something that a comedian says even on a talk show can still get him in trouble in a courtroom. For one thing, there is always that old principle that "a person is not allowed to murder another's reputation in jest." But that's not the situation we have in this lawsuit, it seems.

In life, it is said that you win some and you lose some, and Trump certainly had a big win in that defamation case against Miss Pennsylvania. But there are real differences between the case he won against the beauty queen and any possible defamation case that he could bring against the comedian here. The biggest difference is that the beauty queen made a statement of fact that the pageant was rigged, which turned out to be a false statement. It is easy to imagine the serious damage that such a rather ill-advised statement can cause to the reputation of both the Trump Organization and the competition itself. Consider the context of the two statements: The Miss USA Competition is a serious event where folks win money, careers are made, role models emerge, and media interest is high. On the other hand, Maher is a comedian who likely was merely grandstanding or bloviating on another comedian's talk show, a program which opens every weeknight with a traditional stand-up monologue. The two scenarios are vastly different from one another.

In the end, Maher most probably won't end up paying $5 million on Trump's breach of contract case. But between paying his lawyers and going to court in this lawsuit, perhaps Maher has "picked on the wrong marine" and has made a joke that will bring him an unexpected hassle. Despite his likely defeat in this case, The Donald is a tough customer who plays hard ball whenever the whistle is blown in any fight. Since he is not likely to win this case, he will not be in any position to teach the comedian the kind of "expensive lesson" (as he put it) that he taught the beauty queen. Yet, at the end of the day, he likely will have made his point with his lawsuit—a move that some have angrily denounced as an outrageous attack on comedy.

CASE UPDATE: This one was an easy call from the very beginning, and the end result presented no surprises to many except perhaps for the timing of it all. On April Fools' Day 2013, it was reported that Donald Trump had dropped his lawsuit against Bill Maher. Since no one had expected Trump's case to go anywhere and his public defeat was looming, the rather early withdrawal from the fight needed to be accompanied by some sort of explanation. Knowing this, the ever-savvy billionaire portrayed the move as something of a tactical maneuver the obvious implication being that Maher may yet be summoned back to court at some future date.

Trump's lawyer claimed that "the lawsuit was temporarily withdrawn to be amended and re-filed at a later date." Well, the withdrawal marked the end of the case for good. Yet, it is worth observing that litigation can be a pretty expensive business that can sometimes be weaponized against a rich litigant's opponents. Speaking of strategic attacks on comedians by money bags with deep pockets, Maher's position here recalls that of another comedian, John Oliver, who was unsuccessfully sued for defamation by another billionaire, Robert Murray, a Trump ally. Despite defeating Murray in that case, both very easily and very early, Oliver reportedly forked over more than $200,000 for lawyers' fees plus a huge jump in his insurance premiums.

*A few years later, on Tuesday November 8, 2016, Donald Trump was elected the 45th president of the United States. And he remains pretty controversial.

DAVID LETTERMAN Has No Private Action Against Alleged Extortionist

New York
November 3, 2009

Last September, Robert "Joe" Halderman, the producer of the CBS show *48 Hours Mystery*, was arrested and charged with allegedly attempting to extort comedian David Letterman of $2 million in exchange for keeping silent about secret facts in the comedian's personal life which would "collapse his world around him" if revealed. According to the indictment, Halderman threatened to expose Letterman's long running affairs with his assistants on *The Late Show*, especially a producer on the show with whom Halderman had just broken up after years of living together. Halderman also was alleged to have put together and shown to Letterman supposedly compromising photos, diary entries, and a proposed screenplay that chronicled Letterman's indiscretions with the staffers of his talk show.

The Letterman ordeal recalls a similar one endured by famed Hollywood singer and actress Liza Minelli in 2004 when her personal bodyguard and assistant M'Hammed Soumayah threatened not only to expose embarrassing details about her personal life, but also to cooperate with her then estranged husband David Gest in the couple's pending divorce action. Prior to the blackmail, Minelli had attempted to offer Soumayah a new employment contract that would lower his salary in line with his reduced schedule of duties. However, Soumayah demanded that Minelli keep him at his old salary of well over $200,000 a year. Fearing serious damage to her reputation from Soumayah's threats of exposure, Minelli actually did make payments for a three-month period during which Soumayah did nothing in return.

In New York State, these actions constitute the crimes of larceny by extortion and attempted extortion, which could land perpetrators behind bars for years even if the damaging information they have on the celebrities (the "goods") happen to be true. In these two cases here, the celebrity victims sought the aid of law enforcement, and the alleged extortionists were arrested. But can the victims also file their own private lawsuits against their tormentors? It is almost intuitive that they ought to be able to do so. But can they really?

The short answer, incidentally, is that they can't, at least in New York. And this has nothing to do with whether they should or should not be able to sue. New York courts have made the call that it would be improper to continue such disputes outside the DA's [district attorney] bailiwick.

Translation: the courts have simply said that there should just be one bite at the apple here and that only the DA gets to do it. Whether this kind of line drawing by the courts is fair or not is a different matter, and at this point only the legislature in Albany can give folks like Letterman and Minelli a private right of action.

But as far as private lawsuits are concerned, there may be a silver lining for celebs who are victims of extortion, depending on the factual circumstances. For example, Minelli was able to convince the court to make Soumayah shut up pursuant to a confidentiality agreement he had signed as part of his employment relationship with her. He had worked as her bodyguard. The agreement required Soumayah not to disclose any personal facts he would learn about Minelli's daily life in the course of his job. Letterman had no such relationship with Halderman. This means that any punch he might want to land against Halderman will have to be delivered outside of civil court.

THE "WEDGIE" COMEDIAN: Crossing the Line Between Comedy and the Jailhouse

Florida
August 8, 2013

Though he's still pretty young, aspiring comedian Charles Ross not long ago learned a simple lesson he should have known all along: that comedy is only about jokes if other people also understand what is happening as a joke, even if they may not like the said joke. And of course, as long as any funnyman involved stays within the boundary lines of the law. Stepping outside the lines drawn by the law can really push things off a cliff and bring unintended consequences for the jokester, including possibly an unexpected visit to the jailhouse. In other words, a bad joke is one thing, but in the real world out there not everything is regarded as a joke—for instance, giving wedgies to total strangers. (For those who may not be familiar with the term, a *wedgie* occurs when someone's underpants bunch up between the person's buttocks. Oftentimes, wedgies are pranks associated with schoolyard bullies and most folks don't think of the wedgie look as "cool.")

This past January in Bradenton, Florida, eighteen-year-old Charles Ross was arrested by the police and charged with battery after one of the visitors at a movie theater in the city reported to the police that Ross had put his hands on him and had given him a wedgie. According to the police report, the twenty-year-old complainant alleged that Ross had grabbed him "by the back of his pants and pulled them up hard." The complainant also stated that while Ross was performing the wedgie on him, Ross had asked him if he wanted to hit him [Ross] and that by Ross' arrangement, the whole incident was being filmed.

Well, just like the complainant himself, the police were in no mood for jokes either, and so Ross was arrested and locked up overnight before being released on bail the next day and given a

181

court date for his battery charge. The police report also indicated that there had been other victims of Ross' misconduct who did not have the nerve to press charges because they were simply too embarrassed to do so.

It is not surprising that the police found other victims of Ross actions on the day he was arrested because apparently doing this kind of stuff was simply the way that Ross rolled at the time. He was something of a well-known gadfly in the area who shocked unsuspecting strangers with various embarrassing pranks, which were then posted on his YouTube site *RossCreations*. Some of the pranks he had pulled over time and posted on his site are as follows: kissing total strangers to their utter shock and embarrassment; faking "trust" falls with strangers by walking up to them, turning his back toward them and challenging them to catch him as he falls backward with his arms stretched sideways; asking strangers to scratch his back; doing handstands over strangers who were bikini-clad women laying on the beach; plumping himself down on the laps of strangers sitting on park benches; dressing as a pink pig, then running up to people and leaping onto their backs; and many more.

Both Ross and the police put different spins on exactly what Ross does on his YouTube site. While Ross prefers to style his actions as "pranks," the cops see them as Ross merely "creating situations in order to harass and annoy people." Regardless of how anyone sees what he does, Ross's antics have elevated him to a celebrity on the internet. And, as one might predict, given the times we live in, Ross's celebrity profile has grown even higher with his current police trouble: shortly after the arrest incident, his YouTube channel reportedly received over 50,000 new viewers, taking his total count to well over five million viewers.

As it happens, Ross isn't the only comedian who mixes his comedy with practical jokes. Others do it too, on occasions, including even veteran comics. Perhaps many will recall the media story from 2010 when comedy legend Richard Belzer jokingly put his hand on the shoulders of an Apple Store employee in Midtown Manhattan. Belzer ended up having to explain to the police why his frolic was not enough to get him arrested and charged with harassment. He was able to talk his way out of the mess with help from the store's video surveillance recording. So, practical jokes can sometimes get really tricky. And this is what makes this case quite a teachable moment for comedians who don't confine themselves to doing their act onstage and who try to involve strangers in their act without the prior consent of such strangers. The biggest risk here is that those strangers may not share the comedian's sense of humor and that's where the trouble breaks out.

When a comedian is performing onstage, he can pretty much say whatever he wants and can get away with so much stuff without running into trouble with the lawman. But getting into other people's spaces without their consent or, worse, actually touching them takes matters way outside the free speech zone and creates a whole different ball game.

Speaking of the law, the charge against Ross here is battery. A person commits battery when he deliberately makes physical contact with somebody else without any lawful justification. For the physical contact to be regarded as battery, the touching that occurred has to be rather 'offensive' in nature. This of course means that the person who made the contact (or did the touching) did not have the permission or consent of the other person to touch that other person's body; the other thing here is that the person who did the touching did not have any lawful excuse for the touching. One can imagine from this explanation that when a cop, for instance, puts his hand on somebody during an arrest, his power of arrest as a cop gives him his lawful excuse to touch folks in that manner and still not be guilty of battery. This also means that doing things like giving a woman an unwanted kiss can be regarded as battery.

So, where does all this leave Ross and his cop case? Well, this one is pretty easy: the lawman got him! With respect to proving battery, this is the easiest case ever, as Ross himself has done the prosecutor's job for him: he literally filmed himself committing a crime. In doing so, Ross himself might as well have been an investigator working for the DA's office. Pretty boneheaded thing to do! Luckily for him, it's only a misdemeanor battery charge, but still he will likely get a criminal record.

In a place like New York, for instance, Ross might also have been hit with a 'harassment' charge for his actions. In this case, the prosecutor is required to show that the accused person intentionally harassed, annoyed, or alarmed somebody else by striking, kicking, shoving, or making some other physical contact with that other person. Usually, cases requiring a person to prove exactly what another person intended to do are tough ones to crack because it's not easy to read other people's minds. Yet for a guy like Ross here, this is pretty cold comfort because there is little doubt from his actions that he intended to do all of those things that the law of harassment says should not be done.

Aside from bringing a police case against him, some of the victims of Ross' pranks could also have opted to just go after him on their own, in civil court, that is. They'll be looking to hit him in his wallet by seeking damages against him. The most obvious ground on which to seek damages against him would be "battery," which is also a tort, or civil wrong. And the requirements for winning a battery case in civil court is pretty much the same as what is required in criminal court, as already described above.

And as long as we're in civil court, the victims of his prank could also decide to sue him for damages for another tort, which is less commonly talked about than the others, perhaps because it is generally harder to make such a claim stick. Still, the claim is available. This tort is called "intentional infliction of emotional distress." And this kind of claim can be filed by any person who alleges that the actions of another person toward him are so outrageous and so way out of the ballpark that they simply should not be tolerated in a civilized society.

Needless to say, because of the requirement of outrageous behavior on the part of the offender, petty annoyances or trifling misbehaviors likely won't make the cut with this kind of claim. And the standards for judging outrageous behavior are usually the standards of the community where the thing happened. It's fair to say here that most of the kinds of pranks that Ross pulls on his shocked victims would be considered by most folks to be outrageous, whether we're talking about suburban Bradenton, Florida, or even Times Square in New York City.

In the end, cases like this one, although pretty silly when one comes to think about it, can only be a lesson to people when considering where the lines are drawn between doing comedy and invading other people's lawful space. Ross himself reportedly admitted that this "ended up not being one of his best jokes." Well, actually, it isn't even a joke at all. It's flat-out law breaking that certainly exposes him to unnecessary liability. To be sure, dumb stuff like this would sooner have him sitting in jail than becoming the next superstar on Comedy Central. So, seriously, it's time to wise up: Knock it off, already!

PUTTING SATIRE ON TRIAL? The Mayor, the Comedian and Public Safety

Louisiana
July 27, 2021

Satire is a well-recognized institution in our society, and culture and public safety is, well, a necessity. And they each travel in their lanes. But when these two lanes happen to cross paths how do we manage the encounter so we can allow them to continue to co-exist in our world? This is the tricky question at the heart of the legal battle between the New York-based comedian John Merrifield and Josh Guillory, the mayor of the City of Lafayette Consolidated Government in Louisiana.

In summer 2020, the comedian created two fake events on his Facebook page announcing planned protests by ANTIFA (militant left-wing activists who oppose far right groups) in two Lafayette, Louisiana locations, one in the high-end community of River Ranch in July and the other at the Acadiana Mall in August. In response, the city government deployed a large number of police officers, vehicles and other resources to both locations to tackle the situation. However, since the whole thing was a hoax, no protests in fact occurred at either location.

Later that summer, the city sued the comedian to recoup its purported expenses, claiming that the "hoaxes have cost the city considerable sums of money both in investigating and responding to the hoaxes." The city's said expenses were tallied at less than $75,000.

In a defiant response, the comedian refused to apologize and vowed to fight the lawsuit, claiming that his actions were merely those of a satirist and comedian who created satire events on a comedy meme page on two occasions. "Fool you once, shame on me. Fool you twice, shame on you," he noted. Merrifield, who is a Lafayette native, explained that he meant to highlight how police treat some groups differently and "fail to offer the same protections to the working poor and mentally ill people of color such as in the case of Trayford Pellerin's execution." (The week before the date of the second event in August, protests had taken place at the Acadiana Mall, over the police killing of Pellerin, a Black man.)

So, what's the deal with what the comedian did? Is this allowable "satire, under the First Amendment, as he claims, or is it some sort of mischief intended by the comedian to cost the city some money, as the city's lawsuit suggests?

As we commonly understand it in our society, a work of "satire" uses humor as a vehicle to critique, ridicule or scorn the actions of someone or some institution in the society; as a result, most acts of satire tend to have the purpose and effect of correcting the behavior of the person or institution that is the target of the satire.

Merrifield said that he intentionally worded the announcement in such a way that "anyone with discernment" would know it is a joke and that no reasonable person would think otherwise. The said event post invited only "card-carrying" ANTIFA members and also said things like "arms optional, legs encouraged."

For its part, the city admitted that it knew ahead of time that the whole ANTIFA affair was a hoax but deployed the law enforcement resources anyway even though no actual protests were occurring on any of the two event days in question. The city also said that the officers who were deployed to the scenes were on their regular duties rather than any special duty connected to the planned protests. If this is all there is to all this, then it's game over since the two sides can be said to be on the same page: the comedian intended his post to be understood as a joke and apparently the city did in fact understand it as a hoax by a comedian.

Except that the city offers some explanations for its actions; it said it was acting in response to phone calls from allegedly "concerned citizens" who believed the planned protests were real rather than fake (the city also referenced the comedian's own mother as one of those who believed the planned event was real). Additionally, the city said that it chose to deploy police to the scene in order to pre-empt the actions of any counter-protesters at the planned event (here the city references the posts put out by right wing group Right Side Millennials who were threatening to oppose the planned event).

Given all this, the big question in this case is whether the actions of the city were "reasonable" under the circumstances, considering everything it knew at the time. If the answer to that question is yes, then the city's odds of winning the lawsuit increases. Here's another way to look at it: if the city had not taken the steps that it took, would the city have been considered "negligent" in not doing so. (In common parlance, "negligence" here means the city not taking proper or necessary precautions to safeguard public safety in the circumstances then existing.) If the steps taken by the city are perceived as justified in the eyes of a "reasonable person" looking at the circumstances faced by the city at the time, then the city might have a remedy against the comedian, including, for instance, recouping its expenses from the situation.

If that is the case, it likely won't help the comedian too much to say that his actions were intended as satire. The simple reason here is a practical one: under the law, public safety, just like public health, trumps humor. (Recall, for instance, all the lockdowns and other restrictions imposed on so-called non-essential businesses, including comedy clubs, during the COVID-19 pandemic on grounds of public health and safety.) The other possible problem for the comedian here is that his attempted satire is not your grandfather's good old satire that stays within our traditional understanding of satire. In other words, it's not like a cartoon or some similar critique of a person or a thing, but instead his actions were rather more aggressive with potentially practical consequences. In a manner of speaking, maybe he was somewhat more activist than critic.

Yet the saving grace for Merrifield is that, by its own admission, the city did in fact understand his posts as a "hoax" that was not real. Plus, there were indeed no actual protests at any of the two locations of concern to the city which, by the way has admitted that the presence of its police officers and sheriffs at those locations was done as part of their regular duties rather than as a special effort to safeguard public safety in response to the situation created by the protests. Since a case like this one turns upon a balancing of the facts and circumstances of the case, it therefore seems likely that the actions of the city will not be considered as "reasonable" or "justified" under the circumstances. The city is only allowed to do what is reasonable rather than what is overly cautious under the circumstances it faced at the time. If the city overshoots the mark in its own assessment of the situation beyond what a reasonable person would do, then the comedian cannot be liable for the city's error of judgment.

All things considered, the odds of winning in this case seem to tip clearly on the comedian's side. And so, one may wonder whether pursuing a lawsuit against a struggling comic who probably isn't a deep pocket is the best use of the city's time and resources at a time that the pandemic is still around. However, one plausible way to explain this situation is that by forcing Merrifield to spend money defending the lawsuit, Josh Guillory's city (as the richer party) might be looking to teach the comedian a lesson not to "mess with" the city. Such a game plan will be aiming to set up a "teachable moment" on the acceptable boundaries of satire in contemporary society. Needless to say, these are pretty interesting times in satire.

DIVVYING UP THE DOLLARS
FROM COMEDY WORK

CHAPTER SIX

DIVVYING UP THE DOLLARS FROM COMEDY WORK

Comedy isn't just fun and games anymore. Actually, it has become big business too, especially now in the 'golden age' of comedy. It is common knowledge that divvying up the money made in any business is usually one of the major sources of disagreement among the participants – and the comedy business is no exception. This section deals with the ways in which the divvying up of money that arises from comedy work is handled, whether we're talking about money from a comedy movie, a sitcom, or from the actual running of a comedy club. Most of the cases in this section involve situations in which the courts have been invited to sort out the points of disagreements between the collaborators in various kinds of comedy enterprises. And just like the cases in Chapter One, the cases in this section also demonstrate the importance of clearly written agreements in these situations.

These situations range from the fight over the residual income from the 1990s hit sitcom *Home Improvement*, to the sibling rivalry situation at the storied Los Angeles venue The Comedy Store.

The only exception among the cases in this section, one not involving an actual court case is the Louis CK fame and fortune discussion, which uses the comedian's success story as a case study to show the ways in which the law allows the modern comedian (and indeed other successful entertainers) the leeway to make more money with their names, or to try to control who else can make money from their names even after they die. Of course, this also shows just how difficult it can be for the rich and famous in certain situations to prevent free riders from cutting in on the money flowing around the rich and the famous.

* * *

BEING LIKE LOUIS CK: The Modern Comedian, Fame, Fortune, and the Law

United States
December 22, 2013

Comedy today is at a "golden age," and Louis CK is one of the greatest beneficiaries of this new age in comedy. And Louis doesn't shy away from acknowledging his good fortune: "The amount I get paid by these promoters is crazy…I could make $100,000 in a night," he said about two years ago to *Maxim* magazine. Aside from the big fees he commands when he actually performs his act, Louis CK can also rake in a ton of money from just his massive fame alone. This is what would happen when he, say, endorses a product or licenses other folks to use his name for whatever it can fetch them. And the picture gets even more rosy thanks to the way the law has changed over the past thirty or so years. This means that even after he passes away, the party continues, so to speak: His daughters or whoever controls his estate can keep using his fame to make money as if the guy's still around.

But can anything go wrong with this enviable picture of a gravy train? For instance, suppose folks who are not connected to Louis CK and who do not have his blessing want to get in on the money action anyway by trading on the comedian's fame, can Louis CK stop such guys? (You can use the term 'freeloaders' for these guys if you like.) Or, if he's no longer around, can his "heirs and assigns" (you know, his kids and other folks to whom he may have given the right to control the use of his fame) stop the freeloaders? Well, the short answer is that, thanks to the 'free speech' clause of the First Amendment, these freeloaders can get away with it, if they are smart enough in the way they go about it. Of course, with things like this, the devil is in the details. And the real headache for everyone involved is that we're not talking about a black-and-white situation by any means.

By the way, everything we've already said above plus whatever we will say below on this subject applies equally to each of today's successful or famous comedians as it does to Louis CK.

For starters, the ability of a famous person (or celebrity) to control the use of his name or fame by choosing when to endorse products or to grant licenses to others is called the "right of publicity." And here we're dealing with things like the use of the famous person's name, photo, voice, signature, likeness, and anything else about that person's life that has 'commercial value.' We usually encounter this right of publicity power when dealing, for instance, with the use of a person's name in connection with an ad for a product or a service.

As part of the celebrity's control over his publicity package, he can, if he wishes to do so, give or transfer this right to somebody else by way of a contract. In that case, folks who try to mess with this right of publicity will have to answer to the new guy who acquired the right under the contract. In short, the right of publicity is usually so personal to the guy who owns it that if we were talking about goods and services or creative works like books and movies, we'll be using terms like *trademark* and *copyright* instead. Of course, when it comes to the right of publicity, we are dealing with the identity of a person rather than a thing, but the very idea of owning something with "commercial value" is the same in the right of publicity situation as it is with the trademark and copyright situations.

There are several ways in which a famous person's right of publicity could be violated by somebody else. The easiest situation is where someone, for instance, uses Louis CK's name in a product ad without his permission. That obviously would be a violation of his right of publicity, and this is something that any bloke on the street could easily understand. Same goes for attaching the man's name to a comedy show or a music concert that he has no connection with, in hopes of boosting ticket sales from doing so. By the way, it is worth noting that these are the kinds of situations that originally led to the creation of the right of publicity in the first place.

In other areas outside comedy, the right of publicity is taken no less seriously: For instance, when someone tried to sell a plastic bust of Martin Luther King Jr., his family won a lawsuit to put the kibosh to that move. Also, the TV personality Vanna White from *Wheel of Fortune* was able to stop an ad that mimicked her actions by using a robot wearing a blond wig to turn block letters on a game board. To bring the matter closer home to comedy, somebody who goes out there today, for instance, to use the line "Here's Johnny," which evokes *The Tonight Show with Johnny Carson* will probably be shot down for wrongfully appropriating or taking something of value from Johnny Carson.

In the real world, when somebody violates a famous person's right of publicity, the usual remedy is a lawsuit that seeks damages and more. The famous person could, for instance, ask for an accounting of the money or profits made from the unauthorized use of his or her name. The court could also hit the offender with an order of punitive damages, attorney's fees, injunction, and more.

Speaking of how courts handle situations where it is alleged that a famous person's right of publicity has been violated by somebody else, the one case that stands out as a good example is the 2001 case involving *The Three Stooges*, who were slapstick comedy legends from the 1950s and 1960s. In that case, a California artist reproduced charcoal sketches of the Stooges trio (Moe, Larry, and Curly) on lithographs and T-shirts and then offered the drawings for sale to the public. The children of *The Three Stooges* team then sued the artist for a violation of the right of publicity of the Stooges trio, all of whom had died a long time ago. The court agreed with the children and rejected the artist's claim that he was exercising his free speech rights under the First Amendment.

In essence, the court said that because the artist's drawings did not make any kind of 'creative contribution' to the likeness of the trio, it just was not the kind of expression that the First Amendment lives to protect. In other words, since the drawings did not add anything new or fresh to the image of the three men, there was therefore no message of any sort in there, which could have been regarded as some kind of 'expression' of his free speech rights. As the court saw it, the drawing made by the artist (Gary Saderup) lacked any real creativity and was therefore just a flat-out use of the image or likeness of famous people to make money. Well, it is probably not such a bad idea to note here that although it may not be immediately obvious, there is actually a certain downside to the way the court handled this case: Thanks to this kind of approach, the judges are now the guys deciding what is 'art' and what isn't art as well as what is creative enough to qualify for free speech protection and what isn't. Talk about a fuzzy picture and a situation where it is hard to gauge which way the wind is blowing.

Yet that's just the law. Incidentally, the way the court decided the *Stooges* case also answers the question posed above regarding when other folks are allowed to benefit from a celebrity's fame without his permission. To put the matter in lay persons' terms, one can say that if the material in question is 'creative' enough that it can somehow be viewed as containing a 'message', then chances are that it will be regarded as an 'expression,' which is protected by the free speech clause of the First Amendment. For instance, if the artist's drawing in *The Three Stooges* case would have been presented in a way that perhaps made fun of the three slapstick comics rather than simply reproducing their likeness and offering it for sale, the court likely would have accepted it as a 'parody,' which is a form of expression protected under the free speech clause.

Also, it's important to note that contrary to a common misconception by many, the fact that a piece of art bearing the likeness of a famous person is offered for sale to the public, or even that it is mass produced in several copies does not necessarily mean that the work is not a valid expression of free speech rights. Of course, we all know that somebody who is mass producing copies of an image and offering it for sale is in it for the money. Yet, thanks to the free speech law, he is allowed to do so as long as he is smart and creative enough to give the thing the appearance of some kind of a message.

It's said that because celebrities have such a large role in peoples' lives and mean different things to different folks, making use of celebrity images in different "creative" ways is an important form of expression for people. That's why the courts have, for instance, allowed a painting of golfer Tiger Woods to be sold for money without Woods' permission; the courts have also allowed people to sell trading cards that made fun of famous baseball players, again without their permission. To digress a bit here, one might say that comedians, as people who make fun of things in creative ways, just might find this sort of opportunity to be rather interesting.

In the end, one can safely say that when it comes to fame and fortune, the law today offers a changed and still changing landscape to comedians and the wider entertainment community for that matter. The new landscape, which has been emerging over the past one generation has two sides to it: thanks to the "right of publicity," fame today has been made into something of a property right which a celebrity comic can turn into big money at any time. And when he's no longer around, the celebrity is now allowed to even pass this "right" on to his kids and family (just like his car or his house). Yet, thanks this time to the free speech clause of the First Amendment and the whole business about "creative expression," the law also permits some pesky gray areas that make it possible for total strangers to literally ride the coattails of famous comics on their way to grabbing some fortune of their own without anybody's permission. (The same situation applies to famous entertainers in other fields.)

So, can one say that contemporary superstar comics like Louis CK and others have a fair deal here under the changing law? You bet! Here's the thing: first, to digress just a bit, it is true that because of the holes in the copyright law, comedy material (their most vital asset) isn't really protected from joke thieves and can be stolen rather easily. Yet, when they do hit the fame and are rolling in all the fortune that fame brings with it, the law gives today's comedians the kind of big-time protection of their fame and fortune that their predecessors could only have dreamed of.

CASE UPDATE: In the time since the post was published in 2013, Louis CK's position in the industry has taken a big tumble; accordingly, his overall earnings potential has literally fallen off a cliff since then, thanks in large part to what has happened to him since the advent of the #MeToo era around 2017. In that year, Louis CK finally admitted to inappropriately exposing himself to many female colleagues at various places and different times. He had been forced to make the admission after the *New York Times* ran a story on what had, up to that point been a long running rumor that had dogged the star comedian.

Since his admission of wrongdoing, he's been practically blackballed from the industry, with movie and TV projects canceled, including development deals; his TV appearances yanked, and even his past projects were reportedly scrubbed from the archives of places like HBO and Netflix. However, for what it is worth to his story, Louis CK, to the disappointment of not just a few people, won the award for the Best Comedy Album at the 2022 Grammy Awards for his 2020 special *Sincerely Louis CK*, beating out such comedy stars as Lewis Black, Kevin Hart, and Chelsea Handler. Only time will tell if there is a comeback story here.

THE COMEDY STORE: The Money Side of a Sibling Rivalry

California
September 5, 2011

The Comedy Store in Los Angeles is a legendary comedy club with a lot of proud history to it. And it is no stranger to rocky moments either, like its latest in-house brawl. In one word, the top management is at war with each other. Here's what went down: In December 2009, comedian/actor Pauly Shore, one of the directors of the club filed a lawsuit at the Los Angeles Superior Court against Peter Shore, his elder brother and co-director at the club. Pauly alleged that Peter unlawfully got him removed as a director of the club and also denied him access to accounting information on the operations of the club. Both Pauly and Peter are the children of the club's owner, the comedy doyenne Mitzi Shore, who is the third director at the club.

Among American comedy clubs, the Comedy Store literally has a background like no other. For the most part, the Comedy Store 'made its bones' in the heady 1970s when comedy clubs were just beginning to become the new big thing on the comedy scene and were becoming the pathway to fame and big money in the industry. On the credit side, the Comedy Store was the place that fostered the careers of some of the biggest names we remember in comedy today: Jimmy Walker, Richard Pryor, David Letterman, Jay Leno, and Robin Williams. But then again, the Comedy Store was also the place where comedians staged their first labor-union-type strike in 1979 in their fight to start getting paid for their work.

Mitzi Shore, now in her eighties, owns 100 percent of the shares of the club. However, Mitzi is currently suffering with Parkinson's disease and is hardly involved in the day-to-day running of the place. By most accounts, since Mitzi's withdrawal from running the place, Peter has been handling the money with Pauly taking care of booking new talent. Pauly claims that a month before he filed his lawsuit, he had asked to see the company's tax returns, cash flow statements, and cash register details. Rather than give him the information he was asking for, Pauly alleged that Peter refused to turn over the documents and then proceeded to get him fired as a director of the board, using his influence over their sick mother. Pauly claims that Peter exerted "undue influence" on their mother to get him fired from the board.

As one would imagine, the big question here is: Can Peter hang on to the documents and then literally run Pauly out of town... just like that?

Well, not so fast. For starters, a director of a company is a "fiduciary" of the company. (A "fiduciary" is someone in a position of trust and confidence with respect to another person. Under the law, a company is regarded as a person.) Therefore, any of the directors of a company can inspect the books and records of the company as long as they do it for a "proper" purpose. Of course, they also have to follow the procedures laid down for getting access to such company information. A "proper" purpose may be any number of things, for example, to investigate fraud or mismanagement of the company's affairs or even simply to figure out the value of the company's assets.

With respect to removing a director of a company, usually, it is the shareholders (the owners of the company) who would have the power to do so. In the Comedy Store situation, it looks like Peter did manage to get Mitzi to fire Pauly. Since Mitzi owns 100 percent of the shares, she is in fact the true owner of the company and so would have the right to fire any of her directors. So, on the face of it, it seems that the removal of Pauly may well be valid. But then it gets complicated: Pauly has alleged that his removal was procured by Peter's "undue influence" on Mitzi Shore. If that allegation checks out, then Pauly's removal won't look so valid anymore, and can indeed be overturned.

It turns out that proving "undue influence" is going to be the big thing in this case. Under the law, the potential for "undue influence" usually arises in situations where the two people involved do not have the same or equal capacity to make a sound judgment about things. This could be because one person has superior knowledge about the thing in question, for example, a lawyer and his client when it comes to matters pertaining to the law. Or it could be because one of the two people involved in the situation, maybe due to illness or disease, simply does not have a good enough mental capacity or a state of mind that is "sane" enough to enable him or her to make a sound judgment about things. A situation where someone suffers from Parkinson's disease, like Mitzi Shore here, would be the kind of circumstance where the danger of "undue influence" just might exist. Of course, there are other situations.

In each of the many situations where undue influence might exist, the concern of the law is to protect the weaker party (or the person who is under the disability) from fraud or unfair exploitation by the person in the stronger position. The other reason the law intervenes in these situations is to protect third parties or outsiders whose interests might be adversely affected if actions affected by undue influence are allowed to stand. A good example here may be, say, family members who may lose their inheritance under a will because their sick parent decided to change the will and give everything to, say, his girlfriend. Or perhaps people in Pauly Shore's position if his allegations turn out to be true. What the law does is to literally go over such transactions with a fine toothcomb to ensure that there was no overreaching involved.

As noted above, the Comedy Store situation is the kind of situation where the court would usually want to satisfy itself that there was indeed no "undue influence" considering that Peter, the older sibling was the one who is taking care of their elderly and sick mother. Plus, he seems to have gotten Pauly fired right when Pauly asked to look into the money situation at the company. Quite simply, if Peter explains the somewhat suspicious situation to the satisfaction of the court, then he will be fine and Pauly will most likely be out of the game. However, if the court finds that there was indeed "undue influence," then Pauly will have a great day in court: first, the court could decide to overturn his removal and re-instate him as director. And then, the court could also order or compel Peter to turn over to him the documents he was asking to see.

To be sure, proving "undue influence" is no cake walk, not even by a long shot. And in situations like these, no one can say how the court will ultimately decide the case, mostly because of all the back-and-forth of presenting evidence and making inferences of fact, which are all part of the 'cloud and dust' of a courtroom trial.

There's something else here somewhere: Pauly didn't seem to have done such a great job of troubleshooting ahead of time and this is somewhat surprising. He could, for instance, have tried to bring a "guardianship" proceeding seeking to have the court appoint a formal guardian for his mother. That way, since the guardian would be the one making the big decisions on behalf of Mitzi Shore, Pauly, right off the bat, would have eliminated the chance of Peter being able to influence his mother's decision about who takes charge of managing the Comedy Store. That being said, it is not too late yet to do so, and he can still opt to go that route and get a guardian into the picture and simplify matters.

But whatever happens, the Comedy Store has come through so many storms in its checkered history and, as the saying goes, "this too shall pass." Only this time, the court will get to say how that famous house of laughter is managed going forward. Of course, since this is a family business, it doesn't have to be that way and indeed most comedy lovers would be hoping that the Shore brothers can work things out outside the courtroom and in a family spirit. After all, "this lawsuit is just a family feud," as the old comedian Sammy Shore, the family patriarch and original founder of the Comedy Store in 1972, had observed at the beginning of the lawsuit.

CASE UPDATE: Mitzi Shore died on April 11, 2018 and had reportedly appointed Pauly the manager of the legendary comedy club while putting Peter in charge of the family's production company.

The *HOME IMPROVEMENT* Lawsuit: A Messy Feud over a Billion-Dollar Comedy

California
October 12, 2013

Judging by the numbers, the Tim Allen's 1990s sitcom *Home Improvement* is a highly successful show, which has brought in well over a billion dollars and tons of laughter to boot. But from the look of things, the laughter stopped a rather long time ago for the creators of the show, who claim they have been stiffed in the way the pot of gold is being divvied up. Now, they have invited the court to sort out the messy details of the billion-dollar situation between them and the owners of the show, Disney. The Tim Allen comedy ran on the ABC television network from between 1991–1999 and won a lot of awards in its heyday, including the Golden Globes and the Primetime Emmys. As with most successful shows of its kind, *Home Improvement* has been in syndication in many media markets around the country and abroad since it ended its remarkable run in 1999. But first, here's the story:

This past February, the producers (creators-writers) of the show and their various production companies, who claimed that they were profit participants on the show under an agreement, sued ABC's parent Disney in Los Angeles for syndicating the show at "well below the fair market value" and for not consulting with them on the business plans for the exploitation of the show. They alleged that Disney's actions essentially denied them their fair share of the profits arising from the show.

The plaintiffs, Matt Williams, Carmen Finestra, Tam O'Shanter, and David McFadzean also complain of lack of adequate accounting from Disney as well as an improper allocation of the distribution expenses and other charges to the show. In particular, the plaintiffs who were also the showrunners of the series during its eight seasons objected to the syndication of the

206

show to CBS television in the New York market "for no monetary consideration." In their lawsuit, the plaintiffs are seeking damages for breach of contract; breach of implied covenant of good faith and fair dealing, and damages for unfair competition; they also seek the appointment of a receiver as well as an injunction and an order for accounting.

As it turns out, Disney and the *Home Improvement* folks have been down this path before. In the mid-1990s, another lawsuit over the divvying up of money from the show was settled out of court, but not before the dispute led to the creation of new rules about how studios and networks are allowed to make deals with one another when outside profit participants are involved on shows.

This case is no doubt an important one in the movie and TV industries where syndication deals and profit-sharing arrangements between networks/studios and producers and other collaborators are pretty commonplace. The decision in this case could create yet more rules about working arrangements among these entities.

What are the odds of the plaintiffs winning their claims against Disney? Is the law on their side? Well, let's see:

For starters, this entire case benefits greatly from the fact that there is actually a written agreement between the parties, which controls their relationship. That takes a lot of sweaty guesswork out of the picture. In particular, the breach of contract claim that exists in this case makes the existence of a written agreement here an even bigger deal for the simple reason that a breach of contract action by one party essentially accuses the other party of not fulfilling its promises under the agreement.

Of course, because each situation is controlled by the details of the deal, it is obvious that how clearly the terms of the agreement are written and how much they adequately cover all the bases are always the key worries. Naturally, just like any other plaintiffs in a breach of contract case, the producers of the *Home Improvement* series must first show that they have performed all their own obligations under the contract itself. At first blush, it looks like meeting this requirement should be a breeze for them, considering, well, that they produced the show successfully for all eight seasons.

The key piece of the breach of contract fight here is the producers' claim that Disney failed to consult with them regarding their plans for the exploitation and distribution of the show. Well, since they are entitled to a share of profits from the show, it sure makes sense that they may bargain for this kind of provision in the contract, as they claim. (By the way, the producers claim in their lawsuit that the agreement entitled them to a whopping seventy-five percent of the net profits from the show, aside from their fees for writing and producing each episode of the show during its eight seasons.)

Needless to say, if the producers of the show were not consulted at all by Disney before the distribution deals were made, then it's an easy case of breach of their agreement. In such a case, the producers would indeed be entitled to the exact 'injunction' or order they have requested from the court. The point of the injunction in this case would be to command Disney not to proceed with any further distribution deals and arrangements without first consulting the producers, as provided for in the agreement.

But if they were consulted in any way at all, then it becomes a different ball game altogether. In this situation the quality of the consultation becomes the issue. For starters, by the producers' own admission, just because they are consulted doesn't give them the final say on exactly how Disney implements whatever distribution strategy it chooses to adopt, or even what particular strategy Disney will choose to adopt. This also means that the right to consultation doesn't give the producers the final word on exactly who Disney chooses to license the syndication rights to and, for that matter, how much.

Yet they are entitled to be consulted and to have their input given its due and proper weight. That brings us to their other claim against Disney for breach of the covenant of good faith and fair dealing. This covenant is an "implied" requirement that the courts read into every contract of this nature regardless of whether the parties have actually written the term into their agreement.

In a situation where one profit participant, such as Disney in this case, controls the decision about who to deal with and how much money to charge in each situation, this requirement becomes even more important in order to protect the interest of the other profit participant who is not at the steering wheel of their joint enterprise. A big part of this requirement is that the party in charge of the decision must do his best to obtain at least a fair market value for the product or service being sold. Of course, it would be great if he can obtain the highest possible value for the deal but, strictly speaking, he is not required to do so. Understandably, this leeway is allowed to the deal maker mostly because of the unpredictable waters of business life, plus the existence of other business considerations that often surrounds each business deal.

A fair market value is required in any event. In this case, one of the big questions is whether the syndication of the show to CBS for no money at all is an unfair undervaluation of the product, as the producers claim. If the series are syndicated in other markets for millions of dollars (as the producers claim), then Disney needs a good explanation for why it sold the series for no money in this particular market. And since the producers are already claiming that they were not consulted prior to the CBS deal, things likely won't look good for Disney if they don't have a good explanation for the deal—one that makes business sense.

As noted above, the plaintiff-producers have also tagged on a request for the appointment of a receiver. In laypersons' language, a *receiver* is someone appointed by the court to collect monies or other proceeds of an ongoing business operation. The cry for a receiver is pretty standard fare in situations like this one where a dispute has broken out between two parties both of whom are entitled to the profits from their joint enterprise. And when we have a situation where one of the two parties is the one controlling access to the monies coming in and is also the one allegedly refusing to render full accounting to the other party, the courts are usually more willing to listen attentively to the prayer for the appointment of a receiver; especially if the party seeking a receiver is also the one that is on the outside looking in, like the producers in this case. To be sure, this case seems like a suitable one that requires the services of a receiver in the meantime, no matter who wins in the end.

Then there is the producers' request for an accounting. Well, in a breach of contract situation, one can safely bet that someone asking for a receiver would also be seeking the remedy of accounting. As it happens, the two hands are often played together by the same person in these kinds of situation. In our case here, the producers are claiming that certain information has been withheld from them with respect to some ongoing accounting exercises, and that in other cases they have been given no access at all to the books and records of the business, in violation of their rights under the agreement. From the look of things, it is difficult to imagine that the court will not assist them to get some accounting in this situation.

In the end, this lawsuit looks like a great candidate for an out-of-court settlement. Considering all the second guessing about whether Disney's business deals make sense, and whether 'fair market value' has been obtained on the deals, and whether expenses have been properly calculated and net profits correctly figured, it looks like matters are in a grey area here and that both sides are locked in a messy fight. The producers still have some heavy lifting to do in this case. Yet, for a party like Disney, it won't be a good idea to let this thing just drag on and, worse, to have the court poring over its ledgers and other business papers, looking for needles in haystacks. That kind of distraction is hardly good for business, especially with a highly successful show that is still in profitable syndication. In a nutshell, it would be smarter in this situation for the two sides to be the ones deciding how to divide the big money between themselves than to let the court do that for them using the blunt instrument of a court order.

CASE UPDATE: On July 23, 2019, just weeks to the start of the trial in September, the parties reached an out-of-court settlement of the six-year-old matter. The terms of the deal were not disclosed.

THE *HAPPY DAYS'* ROYALTY LAWSUIT: Grabbing the Gravy after the Party Ends

California
December 2, 2014

Sometimes in show business, especially when you're dealing with a successful TV comedy, such as CBS' *Happy Days*, just because the party is over (and as some folks like to say, "Elvis has left the building") doesn't mean that the gravy from the show's success may not continue to flow. However, those who are entitled to it still need to be smart enough to locate the said proceeds and then grab it: there's never a shortage of folks in the business world who would keep it from those entitled to get it if those people aren't paying attention. But first, here's the story.

In April 2011, five cast members of the hit CBS comedy *Happy Days* (which ran from 1974–1984 before going into syndication) sued both CBS and Paramount Pictures for breach of contract and fraud. The cast members claimed they were owed royalties of more than $10 million, arising from the use of their images in various merchandising operations by CBS and Paramount. The plaintiffs listed various merchandise lines on which their images were allegedly used, including casino slot machines, T-shirts, lunch boxes, board games, greeting cards, glasses, and DVD packaging. As it happened, the plaintiff-cast members launched the lawsuit after discovering (sometime in 2010, more than fifteen years after the show ended running on CBS) that the *Happy Days* image was being used on casino slot machines and other items. The cast members who filed the lawsuit include the actors Anson Williams, Marion Ross, Don Most, Erin Moran, and the widow of Tom Bosley. (Incidentally, other cast members, such as Oscar-winning director Ron Howard and Harry Winkler opted to stay out of the lawsuit.)

A little over a year later, the parties decided to settle their differences out of court rather than fight it out before a judge.

212

Each side claimed satisfaction with the outcome of the settlement. Though the plaintiff cast members got nowhere near the kind of money they'd asked for in the lawsuit, they won something that's a big deal for them, namely, the right to receive future payments from CBS and Paramount. "We will continue to receive all of the merchandising royalties promised to us in our contracts," said plaintiffs' attorney Jon Pfiffer. For their part, CBS and Paramount claimed that they appreciated the way the court had earlier on dismissed the plaintiffs' "far-reaching claims, which paved the way for an ordinary settlement based on contractual issues." Fair enough!

Perhaps both parties saw the settlement as something of a wash, and for that matter it is always a good thing for each side to see a benefit for itself in any settlement. Yet, it is no big surprise that CBS and Paramount would welcome a chance to settle the case. For starters, their willingness to settle at all says something about the strength of the plaintiffs' case because, let's face it, not many folks in their position would settle a multimillion-dollar case if they thought they could win it rather easily when push comes to shove in court. As a matter of fact, despite a couple favorable rulings from the court, CBS and Paramount ultimately didn't succeed in their attempts to dismiss the plaintiffs' case.

So, anyhow, the case settled. Good for both sides! But the nature of the issues in the case has caused some industry folks who themselves also work with TV studios on comedy shows to wonder how both sides would have fared if the matter had gone to trial on the breach of contract and fraud claims. Obviously, the settlement of this case did not quell their curiosity.

So, perhaps it is well to say a couple things about just what could have been in the case. For starters, the claim of a typical plaintiff in a breach of contract action is that though the said plaintiff has fulfilled its own part of the deal, the other side, by contrast, has not fulfilled its part of the agreement that they both entered into. Naturally, the terms of the agreement are everything

213

in any contract case, especially if the parties are so fortunate as to have a written contract in existence between them.

As one might expect, the clearer the terms of the agreement are, the greater will be the chances of the parties being able to resolve matters in an "ordinary settlement based on the contractual issues," to borrow the post-settlement language of CBS. All that anybody has to do in those situations is to look at the facts on the ground and simply check those facts against what the clear terms of the agreement said should be done whenever those facts exist. Simple as that!

Speaking of contracts with studios for TV comedies like *Happy Days*, the usual practice is for the talents (actors) to secure for themselves a right to share in any merchandising revenues that result from their show, usually through the payment of royalties to them. Often, we're talking about the use of their images or names on merchandise as well as any other use or appropriation of their identity in the stream of commerce. In our case here, it is noteworthy that the plaintiff cast members of *Happy Days* claimed in their lawsuit that, under their written agreement, they were entitled to between two and a half percent and five percent of net revenues from any merchandise out there in the marketplace that bears their images.

That brings us to the fraud claim in this case. In everyday language, fraud means deceit, as in, being deceived by somebody else. For example, if Paul enters an agreement with Jim to give Jim some money if certain things or conditions come to pass, and then Paul willfully fails to tell Jim that those specified things or conditions have indeed occurred, and thereby denies Jim the right to receive the money promised, that would be a case of fraud. To be sure, a case of fraud could happen in a contract situation, either because one party to a contract totally fails to disclose something to the other party to the contract, or because he willfully chooses to disclose incorrect or wrong information to that other person. It is important to mention here that in a contract situation there is usually an implied obligation to act in good faith and deal fairly, and therefore to disclose what is known as "material" information to the other party to the deal. In a situation where the second party (like Jim in our example above) is entitled to money under certain circumstances, letting that person know that those circumstances have indeed occurred is the sort of "material" information that the first party (like Paul in our example above) would be required to disclose to the other party. This sort of implied obligation to act in good faith and deal fairly is usually imposed upon the party who has control of the information, such as CBS and Paramount in our case here, or Paul in the example given above.

Anyhow, as a practical matter, anytime that a breach of contract action is accompanied by a fraud claim, what usually happens is that where the terms of the agreement are clear, and if the facts and circumstances provided for (or anticipated) in the agreement are shown to have occurred, then the court will order the stronger party to render an accounting to the other party. The "stronger" party in these situations is usually the party that is in a "position to know" the facts in question.

In our case here, we're talking about matters like the exact amount of revenues that are coming into the till from the use of images of the *Happy Days* cast members on casino slot machines, T-shirts, glasses, and other merchandise. Needless to say, it is important to ascertain these figures in order to determine just how much monies are due to the plaintiffs in the form of royalties. Also, in our case here, CBS and Paramount would obviously be considered the stronger party when it comes to the kinds of information that is required to be disclosed to the other party.

As it happens, given the stance they adopted at the outset of the case, it is clear that both parties seemed to "get it" when it came to their respective positions in the litigation. The plaintiffs' side claimed that because CBS and Paramount had a 'Don't Ask

Don't Pay' policy with respect to the royalty payments and had barely paid them anything in more than ten years, their lawsuit was essentially a reminder to CBS and Paramount about their obligation to pony up. For its part, CBS acknowledged that the monies were indeed owed and that they were working to resolve the matter.

Considering all the above, it is obvious that if the parties here would have pushed matters to a full trial on the merits, the court likely would have ordered CBS and Paramount to render an accounting to the *Happy Days* cast members regarding all the monies rolling in from the use of their image on all kinds of merchandise. Looking at it objectively, it seems rather smart that the two sides opted to sort out their money matters by themselves instead of allowing the court to do so for them by way of a court order. With a court order, both sides have no say at all over what the court will do, and even more troubling is that they may wind up not liking whatever terms the court will impose on them.

In the end, this particular breach of contract case ended well for everyone, especially the cast members of *Happy Days* who actually had their money on the line. And one might add that the case was of a rather predictable variety, and it ended both when it ought to end, and how it ought to end. Yet the simple lesson here for comedians and other entertainers alike is also a lesson that is not always heeded.

First, it is important to draw up a good agreement with clear and easy-to-understand terms. But then it is not enough to simply acquire a right to receive benefits under an agreement. It is also important to watch out for occasions when that right might materialize so that the right can be enforced. (As noted above, the plaintiffs-cast members claimed they first discovered the use of their images on the casino slot machines only in 2010 some fifteen-plus years after their show ended.) Again, this suggests that just because the other side may be required by law to disclose beneficial information to their counterparts does not necessarily mean that they will in fact do so. For all sorts of reasons, including sometimes a greedy desire to simply hang on to other people's money, the other party might simply choose not to do so. Long story short, in the brave world of business, sometimes when you snooze, you lose.

THE INTERSECTION CRISIS— COMEDY AND OTHER PEOPLE'S LIVES

CHAPTER SEVEN

THE INTERSECTION CRISIS— COMEDY AND OTHER PEOPLE'S LIVES

It takes a certain kind of individual to be a comedian. In attempting to describe comedians, the word *weird* is one that often gets thrown around by people. Another common word used to characterize comedians is *attention seeker*. But, as one might ask, why are comedians the way they are? Is it perhaps something in their background? Well, as many commentators, including a lot of comedians themselves have pointed out, comedy generally comes from a place of enormous pain, as a result of which the very art of comedy itself does become a way of dealing with the pain, a form of therapy in a sense.

Thus, it appears that comedy probably isn't a job for most normal people. In executing their craft, comedians tend to zero in on and get off on things in the everyday life of society that most normal folks either don't notice or are so uncomfortable with that they generally would rather not talk about them. Aside from being so different from others, comedians also tend to see things in somewhat more similar ways with each another: they are more like each other than like the rest of us.

This section deals with the various ways in which people from other worlds handle their relations with comedians, whether on a professional or personal level. These rather awkward intersections cover such diverse situations as the judicial authorities of New Jersey acting in the "Joking Judge" case to prevent a guy from serving as a judge while moonlighting as a comedian or comedian Sunda Croonquist irritating her in-laws with her disclosures of family matters onstage. We see the same situation with British comedian Louise Reay being sued by her ex-husband for talking about their failed relationship in her shows, as well as with the ex-wife of another British comedian Stephen Grant making the same demand of him during their divorce proceeding. "I think people who go out with comedians are well aware that is where a lot of material can come from," Grant insists. Oh well! On to the cases . . .

* * *

THE NEW FRONTIER: What If a Comedian Is Also a Judge?

New Jersey
April 9, 2013

Comedy can be pretty fascinating stuff, and it is especially so nowadays that comedy is such a big influence on the pop culture. Yet, it can also be pretty controversial. At the time of this writing, the New Jersey Supreme Court was set to rule on whether a guy who serves as a judge can also work as a stand-up comic. The case reached New Jersey's high court after the committee that oversees the work of judges in that state decided that Vince A Sicari, a municipal judge in South Hackensack, New Jersey, who also works as a comedian under the name of Vince August, cannot continue to work as a comedian.

The committee based its decision on the ground that for somebody to work as both a judge and a comedian would create a conflict with his duties as a judge. (In the interest of full disclosure, I must state here that in addition to being a comedy industry reporter and blogger, I'm a lawyer and a friend of Vince August's. But to be clear, I am of the view that Vince August the comic should not have to resign his position as Judge Sicari just so he can continue working as a comedian.)

Despite his life in the path of the law, Vince August, even by his own admission, has had a longstanding passion for comedy and thus far he has come a long way in the game: Today, he not only performs regularly as one of the headline acts at Caroline's on Broadway, one of the best-known comedy clubs in New York City, he also works as a warm-up act on one of the most famous and influential comedy shows on TV, *The Daily Show with Jon Stewart* on Comedy Central.

In their bid to force him off the comedy stages, the main worry of the ethics committees' who supervise the conduct of the judges in

New Jersey is that Sicari's work as a comic could cause folks who appear before him when he sits as a judge to worry that he might be biased against them. In addition, given the association of stand-up comedy with weird behavior and the act of just 'joking around,' the ethics committees also worry that a judge moonlighting as a comedian would lower the dignity of the office of Your Honor, the judge.

Well, to be sure, being a judge at any level of the court system is pretty serious business and it is not surprising that the society sees it fit to put judges on a pedestal and to slap a whole bunch of restrictions on their conduct. Therefore, the concern of the ethics committees is a legitimate one and nobody should knock them for doing their job. For starters, there is some concern about the so-called slippery slope, something lawyers are quite familiar with. In this particular case, the slippery slope logic will go something like this: If a judge could moonlight as a comedian, then why shouldn't a female judge, for instance, be able to moonlight as a stripper, as long as she doesn't tell her customers that she's a judge during the day.

Plus, all talk about slippery slope aside, when a judge works as a comedian, there is an additional angle to the picture that, frankly, would not quite exist in the case of, say, a judge working as a stripper and maybe dancing quietly on a customer's lap or even a judge simply moonlighting as a shill on a product commercial. It just so happens that comedians draw a lot of material from the events in their daily life and as a municipal judge in New Jersey, the folks who would often appear before Judge Sicari would be folks involved mostly in traffic violations and disorderly conduct charges, including folks who got drunk or got into barroom fights; played their music too loud; maybe smacked their wives around; urinated in public; menaced a wedding party; unduly threatened law abiding visitors to a public park; gambled illegally and other stuff like that.

And anyone familiar with comedians can easily imagine how these situations could provide any comic with a huge treasure trove for comedy material, just the kind of stuff that the ethics committee would worry about. And they should. (In the example above, it is obvious that neither the judge moonlighting as a stripper nor the judge doing a product commercial on the side would enjoy this advantage of being able to use funny material from their courtroom work in their respective extracurricular activities.)

But that's not what we have in this case. Not even close! In situations such as this one, where things that people worry about may or may not happen, the devil is always in the details, as the saying goes. In a nutshell, the situation with Vince August is completely different, and the way he has handled matters in general should not provoke any worries from the ethics committees at all. As a result, this case deserves to be treated in a different way than other cases where judges are engaged in extra-curricular activities.

From all indications, Vince August has taken great pains to keep his two lives separate and apart from one another. What exists between his life as a judge and his life as a comedian is nothing short of an airtight Chinese wall. First, he goes by a different name onstage as a comedian than his real name as a judge. When he does his comedy routines, he never uses any materials from his life as a judge or makes any jokes that might even remotely suggest that he is a judge. Instead, he bases his comedy routines on his own personal experiences from other spheres of his life that have nothing to do with his being a judge—for instance, his family upbringing.

Unlike many a comic and despite the almost irresistible temptation to do so, August appears to have scrupulously stayed away from using any material from his life as a judge who regularly deals with matters such as traffic violations and disorderly conduct cases. In so doing, he seems to have given up a vast treasure of 'source material' that most comedians would kill to get their hands on.

So far, there is no record that anyone one who has attended any of his numerous comedy sessions over the years learned from anything he said onstage that he does have another life as a judge. In fact, there is an equivalent scenario that one can draw here: When Vince August works as a comedian, the odds of folks recognizing him as a judge are the same as their odds of recognizing him as a judge if he were riding a New York City subway train in civilian clothes.

So, as it turns out, this is not one of those extracurricular engagements in which a judge has brazenly ignored or blithely disregarded the decencies of his judicial office in the pursuit of an extra buck. Not at all! And to get more specific, this is not like the sort of situation where a judge tries to supplement his income with a paid outside gig by, for instance, shilling for Shredded Wheat or Kellogg's Corn Flakes in some product ad. And speaking of judicial post, August's work as a judge is so small that it is actually the short end of his long career stick: He only works part time as a judge and receives a paltry $13,000 per year for his trouble. August spends the vast bulk of his career time working as a comedian and getting paid as such.

In context, a work life of such small proportion ought not to create any real worries about setting a bad example for other career judges: And from the look of things, especially from his busy life as a comedian, it does not seem too much that August is in line for higher office in the New Jersey judiciary. Because of this, there is little chance that he will attain the kind of high profile as a judge that could make him a bad example for other judges or a 'poster boy' for judges behaving badly.

In the end, this appears to be a case that qualifies as an exception to the rule that requires judges to stay within their proper lanes of activity. And this exception should have been recognized from the very beginning.

In the broader scheme of judges doing extra-curricular stuff, this case is more like a low-flying aircraft that should have been allowed to simply remain under the radar. Unfortunately, the sheer stubbornness of the ethics committees in refusing to allow this small stuff to slide has generated such publicity that the case has now attained a surprising high profile.

With the cat now out of the bag and considering his longstanding desire to keep his comedy and judge careers separate and apart from each other, it is hard not to come to the conclusion that Vince August has, perhaps, been unfairly treated in all the brouhaha surrounding this case. Yet, when it comes to doing the right thing, it's always better to do it late than never. In that spirit, it is strongly recommended that the New Jersey authorities simply give this one case the pass it deserves and just move on. It's time to get over it!

CASE UPDATE: Success in this particular case always seemed like a long shot for the comedian-judge. Some people had allowed themselves to hope that perhaps the New Jersey Bar authorities just might let this one case slide. But they didn't. On September 19, 2013, the New Jersey Supreme Court ruled that Sicari's work as a comedian is "incompatible" with the role of a judge and that he couldn't continue to work in both capacities.

In its unanimous 7-0 opinion, the court said: "In the course of his routines, Sicari [Vince Sicari, the judge, a.k.a. Vince August, the comedian] has demeaned certain people based on national origin and religion and has revealed his political leanings and declared his dislike for and intolerance for children. The Court cannot ignore the distinct possibility that a person who has heard a routine founded on humor disparaging certain ethnic groups and religions will not be able to readily accept that the judge before whom he or she appears can maintain the objectivity and impartiality that must govern all municipal court proceedings."

In his reaction to the Court's ruling, Vince August conceded the obvious: "I'm not surprised by the result, but I'm very disappointed. I take great pride in being a judge and to give that up is disappointing."

In the end, August opted to resign as a judge and has continued to both practice law and work as a comedian.

SUNDA CROONQUIST: Comedy and the First Amendment

New Jersey
May 17, 2010

Thanks to the First Amendment which protects the right to free speech, America is the best place a comedian could make a living. Just ask comedian Sunda Croonquist: On April 30, she won a court battle against some family members (her mother-in-law, sister-in-law, and brother-in-law) who sought to punish her for her "shtick." Two years ago, these family members sued her in federal court in New Jersey, claiming that her "shtick," which jokes about her life as a half-black, half-Swedish woman married to a Jewish family, had exposed them to public ridicule. One of the jokes that really pissed them off was the one where Croonquist joked that her sister-in-law's voice sounded like that of a "cat-in-heat."

Comedians, especially stand-ups like Croonquist, make a living by making us laugh and the risk of provoking people with their shtick is usually something of an occupational hazard in their world. And there is no shortage of folks who would rather the comedians shut the hell up. Take the mobster who reportedly roughed up Jimmy Brogan at New York's Catch a Rising Star comedy club in the 1970s ("You think you're funny, Kid?") Or the media execs who would yank comedy shows from their networks for causing offense to politicians or people of faith. Recall the controversy surrounding CBS' cancellation of *The Smothers Brothers Comedy Hour* in 1969.

Aside from people who might beat them up or ruin their careers for what they say, comedians also face pressures from folks who just might sue them for a tort called "defamation." A tort happens when somebody does a wrongful act to another person without having a good excuse for that. In a defamation suit, the claim

228

would be that something the comedian has said about the plaintiff has lowered that person's "reputation" in the eyes of other people in the community.

Of all the scares comedians face in their work, the hassles from defamation actions are probably the most serious, because the folks who sue them in order to protect their reputation are doing something the law allows them to do, unlike some other situations where somebody might, say, be trying to get a comedian to shut up. For example, to beat up a comedian for what they are saying may land you in trouble for assault; and to cancel a TV show just because of its shtick could perhaps open the door to a lawsuit for wrongful termination.

But the good news is that it is much harder for a comedian to get in trouble for defamation in a place like America than in pretty much any place else, especially when "public figures" are concerned. A person is considered a public figure either because the person is a public official or because the person is somebody in the public eye, like a celebrity. In dishing out their jokes about people, comedians really do enjoy picking on public figures and they get big laughs from audiences when they do so.

Yet, for a public figure to win a defamation case against a comedian (or anybody else for that matter), it is not even enough to show that the statement happens to be false. The public figure suing the comedian must show that the comedian made the false statement on purpose or that the comedian was so "out to get" the public figure that the comedian simply didn't care when he was making the statement that the statement probably was not true.

However, Sunda Croonquist was sued for defamation not by public figures but by family members.

So, why did she still win? Again, she won because the First Amendment has pretty large wings. "Opinions" are protected by the First Amendment. When a private person files a defamation action against a comedian, the person must show that the comedian

229

presented the offending false statements as "facts" instead of "opinions." This means that the person cannot win if ordinary people listening to the comedian would understand the comedian to be expressing just an "opinion." And here's the rub: when comedians serve up their "shtick," most people would usually not think they are talking about "facts" and serious matters. More likely, people suing comedians are often told to "lighten up" because the comedians are just making jokes to draw a laugh.

The law on free speech has been around for a while and it would have been easy to predict that Croonquist would win her case. One big lesson from it all, though, is that living in a free society can also be uncomfortable sometimes, especially when we may not like to hear what the law allows other people to be able to say. People such as comedians on a roll during a shtick! With protections like these, who can deny that the First Amendment is perhaps the best friend a comedian can count on in a pinch.

THE STEPHEN GRANT SAGA: Marrying or Loving a Comedian

Britain
February 3, 2011

British comedian, Stephen Grant, is a guy who appears to want to wash his family's laundry in public regardless of their wish. Grant separated from his ex-wife in 2007, and while they were going through a messy divorce in 2009, his ex-wife's lawyers tried to have him sign an undertaking that he would not talk about his marriage onstage. It was claimed that for Grant to include such material in his routine could cause "professional embarrassment" to his ex-wife. Grant and his lawyers rejected the proposal and it flopped.

Grant remained defiant throughout, claiming that he had "been absolutely dying to talk about the whole divorce on stage for over two years." As if to give her a taste of things to come, Grant said his ex-wife is "so two-faced it took ages to upload Facebook pictures of her because I had to tag her twice."

And Grant sees nothing wrong with talking about family in his shtick: "I think people who go out with comedians are well aware that is where a lot of material can come from."

What may seem striking in this situation is how the efforts by members of the Grant and Croonquist families to stop the comedians failed. Perhaps even more striking than the failure of their family folks to stop the comedians is the fact that the family situations in both cases were starkly different: in Grant's case the parties were going through a nasty divorce, whereas in Croonquist's case, the parties were still happily married and still are. Yet the comedians are allowed to push their stuff. But when can or will the law stop them?

Given the kind of work they do, a defamation lawsuit is the most obvious way to go after a comedian if one is pissed off at their shtick. A defamation lawsuit is the kind where one person is suing another person for causing injury or damage to their reputation in society. For a comedian onstage, we would be talking about a type of defamation called "slander," which concerns spoken words that can damage somebody else's reputation.

But the catch here is that the statement that is said to cause the damage to reputation must be the kind that lawyers call a "false statement of fact," which means two things: first, the statement has to actually state "facts" not "opinion," and this is where a lot of comedians can totally beat the lawsuit and get off. Because they are comedians doing a shtick onstage, it is so much easier for folks out there to assume they are just kidding around to get a laugh by doing a "parody" of life in society. Most people watching a comedian performing onstage would not take him as "seriously" as they would take, say, a congressman speaking during a House debate on the budget deficit. Second, even if the comedian made a statement of fact, he still wins if the statement happens to be true.

Yet, there is a way to get a comedian to shut up about matters going on at the home front. For example, a future spouse can get him to sign an undertaking to keep private matters private in the event of a divorce—maybe also during the marriage. This could take the form of a prenup, a confidentiality agreement or something similar. It was a smart move for Grant's ex-wife Anneliese Holland to attempt to get him to sign the undertaking to not talk about the marriage in his shtick. The only problem is, she made her move too late at a time when she had no leverage to make him sign such a deal. Grant already had enough "goods" on her for his shtick. What's to stop an ex-husband from advancing his career by perhaps embarrassing his ex-wife who he claims cheated on him?

In the end, Stephen Grant may be something of an odd duck, yet comedians are not exactly like most other people, especially when it comes to saying or doing things that might cause embarrassment to them or to others. That makes it a darn good idea for people who get involved with them to, well, know what they are getting into. Counting on the law to stop the comedians just might not work.

FREE SPEECH vs. PRIVACY: British Comedian Louise Reay Sued by Ex-Husband

Britain
July 29, 2018

As commonly understood, comedians tend to have extroverted personalities. The problem is, though, other people in the private lives of comedians may not be so extroverted themselves and so may rather want their private business kept out of the knowledge of the public. A recent episode in this sort of saga comes from Britain where comedian Louise Reay and her ex-husband Thomas Reay are currently embroiled in a defamation lawsuit that has been framed as a free speech case, despite being accompanied by some menacing invasion of privacy allegations.

In 2017, comedian Louise (Beaumont) Reay, put together a fifty-minute show titled *Hard Mode* in which she purported to discuss issues of censorship and authoritarianism with references to China and the BBC. However, the show also contained references to personal details of her life with her ex-husband, Thomas, the plaintiff in the current defamation lawsuit. Upon learning of the contents of the show (presented at the Edinburgh Fringe Festival and in London), Thomas sent Louise a written complaint demanding that she stop talking about the said matters on her show. He subsequently filed a lawsuit against her over the contents of the show, alleging defamation, and invasion of privacy and data protection. He also sought £30,000 in damages plus costs and an injunction demanding that she refrain from making (publishing) further statements about him.

The ex-husband's side stated that after clearly identifying him, both verbally and in still and moving images, the comedian ex-wife then proceeded to present private information about her relationship with him, which pushed "the entirely false suggestion" that his relationship with her was "an abusive one."

234

Given how commonplace it is for comedians to talk about their personal lives in their work, this lawsuit is such a big deal especially in regard to how a defeat for her in this case might impact the work habits of comedians who think it permissible and safe to include personal life stuff in their material. Should she lose the case, there is an undeniable chilling effect here, whatever the extent. Perhaps perceiving the significance of this factor, the comedian ex-wife Louise Reay, the laureate of the 2015 *Alternative New Comedian of the Year* award, has opted to invoke the camaraderie of her comedy peers by framing the case as a "free speech" matter of immense implication for the comedy community. Thus, she has set up the crowdfunding website GoFundMe for her legal defense, and her comedy peers have rallied around her.

"As standup comedians I believe it's the very definition of our job to talk about our lives and social issues, so this has become a free speech issue, and free speech means everything to me," she said on the crowdfunding site.

Curiously, though, despite her free speech stance, upon initially receiving the other side's written protest, she did remove the offending references to her husband in subsequent presentations of the show.

(By the way, in plain language for simple folk, liability for defamation arises from the making of false statements of fact that injure the victim's reputation in the community.)

How will her free speech defense play out in this defamation lawsuit? Will it fly?

Well, for starters, it is worth noting that her free speech defense to the defamation lawsuit would have fared way better in an American courtroom than in a place like Britain thanks to America's world-famous First Amendment whose goal is to ensure that debate on matters of public interest is "robust, uninhibited, and wide open." Yet even in America, in order to enjoy such free speech protections, the offending statements must not be knowingly or recklessly false. And of course, they must either relate to discussions about matters of public interest or concern public figures and officials. Since her ex-husband, the plaintiff, presumably, is a private person and the facts about his life and their failed marriage are not matters of public interest, she likely would have had trouble mounting a free speech defense over here in America if she would have been an American defendant. So, long story short, her case probably would have been decided over here in America the same way the British courts are going to decide it—that is to say, like a regular defamation case with no frills.

So, without any First Amendment-style interventions, how will this comedian's available defenses play out in an old-style defamation court litigation?

Well, from all indications, let's just say there is some heavy lifting to be done. To this comedian's peril, it seems that while addressing the vexed issue of censorship in society, she rather chose to take her eyes off the ball for a bit and took an unrelated and quite irrelevant dig at her ex-husband. It's interesting here the way she explained referencing her ex-husband in the show: "The main gist of those references was to tell the audience how sad I was that my marriage had broken down recently." Well, let's just say that this emotional component to the matter doesn't seem like a plus to her case.

Yet, being a comedian in a situation such as this, her most obvious line of defense seems to be an assertion that this whole thing was simply a joke being made by a comedian. Her other defense [already foreshadowed in some of her statements] is something of a *de minimis* claim, namely, that we're simply dealing with a mere two-minute portion of a fifty-minute presentation. In perspective, if she can prevail on the first point about it being but a joke, there will be no need to try to rely on the second point about it being but a rather tiny portion of the entire show. Conversely, if she loses that argument, then the two-minute factor won't help her.

However, for her to win the argument on the "joke" front, it has to be clearly shown at least that the references to her ex-husband were both intended and understood as a joke by its listeners or audience. Only problem here, as the other side claims, is that her ex-husband was clearly identified in both still and moving images, which were then accompanied by factual statements about him and his marriage to the defendant which portrayed him as an abusive person.

The ex-husband alleges that these statements of fact were false and thus defamatory. Question is, will the judge agree with the ex-husband's version of the matter, or will he instead think that the statements were just a joke and would have been understood by reasonable people who saw the images and heard the statements as just a comedian making a joke? (By the way, rare though it may be, someone can still be found liable in defamation for a joke, because as the old saying goes, one is not allowed to "murder the reputation of another in jest".)

And then, there is the invasion of privacy claim, which is a straight up "tort" matter that stands separate and apart from the defamation claim. (Under the law, one commits a tort when the person causes harm to other people by breaching legal duties owed to them.) This concerns the right of people to be left alone in their personal spaces. And in terms of a plaintiff proving somebody's liability, this claim seems to be less complicated than the defamation one where arguments about free speech and opinion issues could muddy the waters and create uncertainty. Not so here. In the present case it is alleged that, without the ex-husband's consent, the show (*Hard Mode*) presented personal information about him, together with still and moving images of him plus other information about what he did during the marriage. On the face of it, there seems to be enough ground here for the court to find an unlawful invasion of privacy. That is, if the allegations are in fact proven. Of course, where it is shown that somebody's privacy has been invaded by another, the courts can always issue "injunctions" to get the offender to stop doing the things complained against.

Also, some might be wondering whether it helps her overall case that in subsequent presentations of the show, she did yank the offending portions of the show upon receiving her ex-husband's initial complaint or protest about the matter. Well, aside from showing that she perhaps realized that she was acting wrongfully, the removal of the said offending portions will probably not absolve her of liability for defamation and invasion of privacy if such liability is otherwise found to exist. More likely, in such a situation, it will be a factor in her favor when the court is assessing what damages to award to the plaintiff.

In the end, whichever way this lawsuit ends for this comedian, it will likely rank among the most serious cases anyone has yet brought against a comedian on account of family-related personal information contained in their comic material. The comedian has already stated that she'd go "bankrupt" if she loses the case and it is no laughing matter to her. Certainly, it is pretty smart of the comedy community to be paying such close attention to it. This is a genuine concern that exists on both sides of the Atlantic, make no mistake.

CASE UPDATE: In December 2018, the parties, to everyone's apparent relief, announced the settlement of the case with a short joint statement: "A settlement has been reached, which has resulted in the claimant discontinuing the proceedings. Both parties have agreed to make no further comment following settlement." Expressing her immense relief at the development, the comedian's mom said: "Fighting this lawsuit has been really tough on my daughter Louise and the whole family, and we are incredibly grateful to all the amazing people who have helped us achieve a discontinuance of the legal proceedings and a settlement."

EPILOGUE

In this section, I feel it appropriate to share my hopes for all who will read this book as well as for the comedy industry itself.

Let me begin by recalling some inspiring remarks from one of the earliest readers of my blog, which, as indicated earlier, was the basis for the book. (As it happens, this reader's comments were posted as a reaction to the piece on Garry Shandling, which appears in this book in Chapter One). Her brief but instructive remarks in the "Comments" section of the blog ran as follows: "What a great blog! The legal side of entertainment exposed to the public in a way that makes it understandable. Thanks for your insights."

To the above gentlelady and other readers of my blog, I can only hope that, since the book and the blog don't contain exactly the same information (for instance, the book, unlike the blog, also contains updates plus much additional commentary), they will also find reading the book just as informative and entertaining as they did the blog. I hope the same for all those who will only read the book.

For comedians, I hope that a couple of simple lessons will be their most important takeaways from reading this book. First, it is a pretty smart thing for them to pay a healthy dose of attention to the way that their *working contracts or agreements* are crafted. More specifically, they will do well to appreciate the fact that getting a positive outcome when problems arise down the road in their working relationships, either with one another or with others who engage their services, will often depend on how well and clearly the agreements are drafted. To be sure, the more the courts have to guess at what the words or terms of any agreement means, the less will be the odds of a satisfactory outcome for the person whom the agreement was meant to protect.

Indeed, there is no substitute for an agreement with words or terms that are clear and unambiguous, and this is true whether we're talking about the right of a comedian to work at all on a particular gig, or how much he or she will receive when it comes time to divvy up the money from a successful enterprise—for example, back-end profits, residuals from syndications and related sources, and whatever else. Nor is there a substitute for an agreement that anticipates as much as it can about what could go wrong in the transaction and then proceeds to include the appropriate provisions and stipulations to cover such situations. And, by the way, it is always better to have a written agreement than an oral one. As in any other business, a written agreement makes life a hell of a lot easier than an oral agreement, especially when push comes to shove in court.

We next come to the matter of *free speech* in open societies. In a place like America, the free speech protections granted by the First Amendment is a highly celebrated right among comedians. This is hardly surprising considering that any group of people who make fun of other people and their situations or insecurities, as comedians often do, would need a lot of room for maneuver. And there is indeed a lot of such room for maneuver for comics in America, as the courts have said in the situations discussed in Chapter Two. But increasingly there is what can be seen as a countervailing force to the free speech rights of comedians.

This force is the all-too-familiar "political correctness" phenomenon that we have all around us these days and whose dictates are enforced by the so-called "PC-Brigade" (Political Correctness-Brigade). The PC- Brigade now appears to have morphed into the more virulent "cancel culture" movement, whose partisans are motivated by notions of "wokeness," itself a rather shifting concept lacking precise or readily ascertainable boundaries. Obviously, these campaigners, who have been derided by some as "culture warriors" do not have many friends in the comedy community, since most comedians resent what they perceive as an intrusion upon their right to speak freely in ways that the First Amendment would actually permit them to say.

Yet, for better or worse, we now seem to have become something of a politically correct society that is uncomfortable with "offensive" speech on any number of subjects, whether it is rape, slavery, the holocaust, disability, or whatever else that might wound the sensibilities of others. For what it is worth, there is something to be said for civility, sensitivity, and general decency in a modern society. This means that the longstanding and popular notion among comedians that nothing is off-limits to jokes has inevitably come into serious tension with the mood of contemporary society.

That said, comedy is now like a lucrative business and the show must go on, regardless. Given that contemporary comedians are in the business of selling jokes for a living, if it should happen that for whatever reason, people out there (consumers) don't want to buy certain kinds of jokes anymore, why continue to offer them for sale? The thing is the old comedy ethos that nothing is off-limits to jokes just might no longer be so good for business in our present cultural moment; so perhaps it might be time for some re-consideration here. In any event, I hope the comedy industry not only acknowledges that there is now a genuine debate about the legitimate boundaries of humor in our society, but that it also actively participates in the debate until the right balance is ultimately struck. Doing this will not and should not diminish our appreciation and celebration of the First Amendment in the comedy industry.

Now, how about comedians who *act out physically*, whether onstage or off stage? Well, this one is easy: It's a flat-out bad idea. Fortunately, the facts in this area so speak for themselves that one doesn't need much persuasion to sell this lesson to comedians. Obviously, when a comedian commits an assault on other people or causes damage to another person's property, there are consequences that follow simply because no one is above the law. Besides, unlike the free speech cases, there is no First Amendment-type protection in those situations.

Then there is the thing about comedy and other worlds. Here's my take: I hope that comedy will continue to impact pop culture in a big way, helping to steer our social conversation and debate. Still on the subject of comedy and other worlds, being a lawyer who also happens to have covered the comedy industry as a journalist, I know that "The Joking Judge" case (in Chapter Seven) has provoked a fair amount of discussion among lawyers, and even from non-lawyers, who were familiar with that controversy. I note that the weight of opinion among those familiar with the matter is that the decision of the New Jersey Supreme Court is the right one. But if I may, here's my two cents on that situation: If a judge wants to be a comedian and he can build a good enough "Chinese wall" between the two undertakings, well, I'd say that it's probably OK to let them go ahead. Again, that Chinese wall, it must be emphasized, is very critical and non-negotiable. Obviously, some can, and others can't. For those who can, I'd say, just let 'em!

About the Author

Carl Unegbu is a lawyer and journalist. He currently runs the blog *ocarlslaw.com* and was an editor at news site Comedybeat. com. He also previously hosted the industry forum *Comedy Dialogue*, a quarterly series held in Manhattan's Upper West Side, featuring stand-up comedy performances and panel discussions involving some of the comedy industry's best and brightest talents. Prior to his work at Comedybeat, he was a reporter in New York City, and over the years his articles have appeared in the *Real Deal* magazine, *Gotham Gazette*, *City Limits*, *World Policy Journal*, the *New York Review of Magazines*, *Leverage* magazine, *Journal of International Arbitration*, *Reuters Forum Journal*, and the *New York County Lawyer* newspaper.

Carl studied journalism at Columbia after graduating law school at the University of Miami. Before being admitted to the New York bar, he served as a law clerk at the International Court of Arbitration, Paris, and then practiced law in Miami. He currently lives in New York City and volunteers his free time for community development and civic affairs in his Manhattan neighborhood.

Printed in the USA
CPSIA information can be obtained
at www.ICGtesting.com
JSHW012023211223
53995JS00009B/33